Joy White goes boldly where no sociologist has previously dared to venture. She takes us inside the social and cultural habits of the Grime scene's young artists and entrepreneurs. Her insightful, detailed exposition of their creative and commercial worlds demonstrates how the politics of race and culture are evolving in Britain and even suggests how hope and dignity might be salvaged from the incorrigible chaos of neoliberal capitalism.

Paul Gilroy, *Professor of American and English Literature,*
King's College London, UK

Urban Music and Entrepreneurship

Youth unemployment in the UK remains around the one million mark, with many young people from impoverished backgrounds becoming and remaining NEET (not in education, employment or training). However, the NEET categorisation covertly disguises and obscures the significance of the diverse range of activities, achievements and accomplishments of those who operate in the informal creative economy.

With grime music and its related enterprise a key component of the urban music economy, this book employs the inherent contradictions and questions that emerge from an exploration of the grime music scene to build a complex reading of the socio-economic significance of urban music. Incorporating insightful dialogue with the participants in this economy, White challenges the prevailing wisdom on marginalised young people, whilst also confronting the assumption that the inertia and localisation of grime culture results from its close links to NEET 'members' and the informal sector.

Offering an ethnographic and timely critique of the NEET classification, this compelling book would be suitable for undergraduate and postgraduate students interested in urban studies, business, work and labour, education and employment, ethnography, music and cultural studies.

Dr Joy White is a postdoctoral researcher whose interests include enterprise, grime music, social policy, mental health and well-being.

Routledge Advances in Sociology

For a full list of titles in this series, please visit www.routledge.com/series/SE0511.

Urban Music and Entrepreneurship

Beats, rhymes and young people's enterprise

Joy White

Routledge
Taylor & Francis Group

LONDON AND NEW YORK

First published 2017
by Routledge
2 Park Square, Milton Park, Abingdon, Oxon OX14 4RN

and by Routledge
711 Third Avenue, New York, NY 10017

Routledge is an imprint of the Taylor & Francis Group, an informa business

British Library Cataloguing in Publication Data
A catalogue record for this book is available from the British Library

Library of Congress Cataloging in Publication Data
Names: White, Joy, 1962– author.Title: Urban music and entrepreneurship : beats, rhymes and young people's enterprise / Joy White.
Description: Abingdon, Oxon : Routledge, 2017. | Series: Routledge advances in sociology ; 189 | Includes bibliographical references and index.
Identifiers: LCCN 2016022784 | ISBN 9781138195462 (hardback)
Subjects: LCSH: Music entrepreneurship–England–London. | Music–Social aspects–England–London. | Youth–Social conditions–England–London.
Classification: LCC ML3917.G7 W5 2017 | DDC 306.4/842409421–dc23
LC record available at https://lccn.loc.gov/2016022784

ISBN: 978-1-138-19546-2 (hbk)
ISBN: 978-1-315-63839-3 (ebk)

Typeset in Times New Roman
by Wearset Ltd, Boldon, Tyne and Wear

Printed and bound in Great Britain by
TJ International Ltd, Padstow, Cornwall

This book is dedicated to Nico Ramsay
5/12/1996–17/2/2016
'Young blood, forever in our hearts, forever in our souls,
in our minds.
RIP Nico'

Contents

Illustrations

Figures

Tables

Acknowledgements

I would like to acknowledge the financial support of the Independent Social Research Foundation (ISRF). To all of my informants, the people at the heart of this book, who were so generous with their time, I extend my heartfelt thanks. I am extremely grateful to Paul Gilroy, who took time out of his busy schedule to offer insightful and helpful comments along the way. I would also like to express my appreciation to Joel Lazarus for his careful reading and constructive feedback on the early drafts. Towards the end of writing this book I experienced a family tragedy. When a young life ends, there really are no words to describe it. Theo Ramsay's tribute to his brother, Nico, says it in a way that I cannot. So thank you, Theo, for giving me permission to use the lyrics from *Better Place* (SBTV: Music 2016) in the dedication to my dear nephew. This book comes out of my PhD research, and my former supervisors, Steve Kennedy and Gauti Sigthorsson, gave a listening ear when needed. The University of Greenwich provided a quiet space to write and library facilities. Finally, I would like to thank my family (way too many to mention), my good friend, Lindsey Bourne, and my daughter, Karis Duncan, for their unwavering encouragement during the writing of this book. Even though you were not always physically present, your positive vibrations were keenly felt and much appreciated.

Reference

SBTV: Music, 2016. *Lil Nasty | Better Place (Plaistow) [Music Video]: SBTV*, Available at: www.youtube.com/watch?v=FMPJDwkqbwE [accessed 22 April 2016].

Part I
Foundations

Setting the scene

My starting point for this project was urban east London in 2007, and the primary research phase continued through to 2012. During this timescale the perceived rise in antisocial and violent behaviour among disaffected youth was at the forefront of public and political consciousness. There was a heightened anxiety about gangs and turf or postcode wars, a constant flow of media reporting and government reports supported the common sense view that this was a worsening inner-city problem that impacted on ordinary citizens (Sherwin 2007; Curtis 2008; journeymanpictures 2008; Rose 2008; Panorama 2009). This fear was based on real events; for example, in a six-week period in early 2007 five teenagers were killed: James Andre Smartt-Ford, Michael Dosunmu, Billy Cox, Kodjo Yenga and Adam Regis were stabbed or shot in separate incidents in London (Mail Online 2007). From 2007 to 2008, a reported twenty-seven teenagers were killed in London (Stickler 2008). Music, particularly the lyrics from grime music, was often seen as part of the problem. It appeared that grime offered a medium for young people to go to war with each other, activating conflicts over territory, reputation or gang membership.

A significant and far-reaching development during the primary research phase was the global recession that began in 2008 and continued throughout 2009. The subsequent economic slowdown contributed to unemployment in the UK rising to levels that had not been experienced since the early 1980s. Long-established businesses, including financial institutions, failed, and the repercussions were compelling at all levels of society. In September 2007, Northern Rock Bank sought an emergency loan from the Bank of England, an act that precipitated images of economic meltdown in the UK as depositors with this bank queued up to withdraw their savings. There was a negative impact particularly on the retail and financial sectors. Furthermore, poor areas, such as those in east London, continued to experience high levels of unemployment. Nationally, the numbers of young people in the NEET category expanded, reaching just under a million in 2008 (LSN 2009). Across Europe, joblessness among the young rose to unprecedented levels; in Greece, for example, 61.5 per cent of young people were unemployed (Taylor 2013).

Young people and unemployment: the impact of a supply-side approach

Leaving school and the family are rites of passage into adulthood. The school-to-work or education-into-employment transitions have been disrupted by structural changes in the UK economy. Whereas in the post-World War II era the majority of young people left school at the end of secondary schooling, now an increasing number stay beyond the compulsory school leaving age. These structural changes mean that fewer entry-level jobs are suitable for young people and therefore the youth employment market has all but disappeared (Furlong and Cartmel 2007; Murray and Gayle 2012). This led to increased levels of youth unemployment (Casson 1979). Youth unemployment rose more in 1980 than it had during the previous decade in total (MacDonald 2011, p. 429). In common with the current economic situation, the 1980s were a time of deep recession, social inequality, severe public spending cuts and civil disturbance. Today, almost one million young adults are unemployed, and tackling the NEET problem has remained a key youth policy since 1997 (MacDonald 2011, p. 430).

Youth unemployment, while it had been a matter of concern in the UK since the last instance of mass unemployment in the 1980s, became a more pressing political issue with the most recent global economic downturn in 2008. At the start of this project, it became evident that young people with further and higher educational qualifications were becoming NEET. In the UK, unemployment among graduates, combined with increased levels of student debt, became a more acute political matter (Harrison 2013; Office for National Statistics 2013). The detrimental consequences for young people not being able to make the transition into adulthood through the usual rite of passage of paid employment are well documented and include lower lifelong earnings, as well as professional and psychological scarring (Kingsley 2011; Lee and Wright 2011; Sissons and Jones 2012).

Mass unemployment in the late 1970s and early 1980s had a critical effect on young people, who as a result experienced wage scarring and limited opportunities. Therefore as individuals they were facing the possibility of life on the margins; at a societal level, large numbers of unemployed, unskilled young people posed an increased risk of creating civil disturbance, as evidenced by the riots in Brixton, Bristol and Birmingham in 1981 (Scarman *et al.* 1982).

The Youth Training Scheme (YTS) introduced in 1983 was one of a number of policy initiatives established to address the problem of unemployment among the young. It was aimed at those of school-leaving age and it offered a one-year (later extended to two years) programme of work experience and training (Mac-Donald 2011). It can be viewed as a precursor to the current government's focus on the creation of apprenticeships for young people as a solution to increased levels of unemployment. Yet the push to drive down the youth unemployment figures avoids one obvious difficulty: the lack of jobs generated by the economy. Instead it focuses on what young people are lacking in employability, attitude and qualifications. Nevertheless, since the 1980s, education policy on attainment and subsequent access to tertiary education, employment and training has had a significant impact on the NEET category.

Education policy and its relationship to the NEET category

The Organisation for Economic Cooperation and Development (OECD) ranks the United Kingdom as one of the richest countries in the world. Britain's continuing prosperity depends on ideas and fresh talent, particularly because globalisation and technological change mean that economic success in the twenty-first century demands 'higher levels of innovation, faster response to change and increased creativity' (Leitch 2006, p. 6). Therefore the challenge for schools and the education system is to focus on and improve economically valuable skills. The expansion of higher education is part of a wider project that sees higher education as a driver for long-term economic growth and national prosperity. Indeed, a well-educated population is still viewed as a prerequisite to the UK being able to compete in a world arena (Sissons and Jones 2012).

The ideological debates over the purpose of education continue apace. The gradual shift from the notion that a quality education for all is a *good thing* in itself to a market-controlled commodity underpins the discussion about whether education means to acquire basic skills required by industry or to understand ideas and use knowledge for broader purposes (Allen and Ainley 2007; Bassnett 2007; Benn 2012). From the 1980s neo-liberal education theories were pushed to the fore at the same time as deep economic recession and intensified global competition. Free market economics began to replace Keynesian economics, and education and learning needs were incorporated into free market economic principles. On the one hand there was widespread discussion regarding new forms of learning and how young people now have a chance to learn in less restrictive environments but on the other hand, there was a strong emphasis on economic competitiveness, privatising of educational facilities and responsibility for learning was now pushed to the learner (du Bois-Reymond 2004). In the UK, an enduring legacy of the economic policies of the 1980s is the groups of alienated and dispossessed people mainly living in inner-city council estates where jobs have disappeared (Tomlinson 2005, p. 106; Sergeant 2009a; Hills 2010). The continued policy changes have been in response to an ongoing concern that the education sector is failing or in crisis. Low educational attainment is a symptom of this.

The New Labour government elected in 1997 retained free market principles of choice and competition. However, there was a shift in terms of New Labour's desire to use education to tackle social exclusion. The 2010 coalition continued with the creation of academies and free schools (institutions funded by the public purse but the curriculum, organisation and staffing lie outside of local authority control). In a further bid to improve educational achievement, the 2015 Conservative government recently announced that by 2020, all schools are to become academies (Stone 2016).

Education is considered a vital institution for the development and growth of the economy, as well as a means to improve life chances and opportunities; yet in the UK, one in six young people leave school unable to read, write or add up properly (Leitch 2006, p. 22; MacLeod 2006; Stevenson and Jarillo 1990). More than ten years of the national literacy and numeracy hour initiatives have had little impact on this statistic (Sergeant 2009b; Shepherd 2010). A recent OECD report ranked England and Northern Ireland 21st and 22nd out of 24 for literacy and numeracy standards respectively (Ramesh 2013). At the same time, there is an ethnic and cultural dimension to this issue, in that a significant proportion of young people from BAME (Black, Asian, and Minority Ethnic) communities (particularly those of Caribbean descent) become NEET (Leitch 2006; Hills 2010). Furthermore, figures from the Office for National Statistics (ONS) suggest that black males aged 16–24 have an unemployment rate in excess of 50 per cent – a rate that has almost doubled since the 2008 recession (Ball *et al.* 2012).

While questions have been raised recently regarding the low academic achievement of white working-class boys (Skidmore 2008; Sergeant 2009b; Bingham 2013), the relative underachievement of pupils of Caribbean descent has been a matter of concern for at least three decades (Richardson 2007). Since the 1970s, growing numbers of black students have variously been classified as 'Educationally Sub Normal' (ESN), 'marginalised' and 'underachieving' (Allen and Ainley 2007; Richardson 2007, p. 137). Furthermore, the attainment gap between black children and their peers is still an issue (Department for Education 2013).

A combination of factors has supported the maintenance of the status quo where young people from poor areas continue to achieve less than their middle-class counterparts (Hamnett *et al.* 2007). These factors include ranking (development of lower tier qualifications), increased competition among schools for the more desirable pupils (those who could take and achieve the higher level qualifications) and the establishment of league tables to identify 'good' and 'failing' schools. This has helped to create what Lucey and Walkerdine argue is a construction of a middle-class, masculine hegemony in which it is acceptable for middle-class boys, but not working-class or black boys, to be laddish and high achievers (Tomlinson 2005, p. 198). It is within this context that schools are able to 'reject, neglect or lose' students who could not attain the five Grade A*–C GCSE passes that act as a gateway to further and ultimately higher education opportunities (Tomlinson 2005, p. 189). Without these qualifications, the risk of becoming NEET increases, particularly for those from poor backgrounds.

East London: the birthplace of grime music

It is accepted that the east London area – specifically the inner London boroughs of Tower Hamlets and Newham – is the birthplace of grime music (Campion 2004; Hampson 2009; Dreamers row 2012; Hancox 2013). Within the urban spaces of east London municipal housing, it is possible to see the residual marks of each community that has come and gone. What remains is a complex and multilayered network of people who draw on diverse cultural and historical backgrounds. These communities operate in a landscape that is changing, but these locations continue to contain sites of poverty and marginalisation. This confluence of people and place created an environment for grime music to emerge, and it is evident that the physical nature of this location has an impact on creative and cultural expression. Adam Krims suggests that urban spaces shape our everyday social and economic behaviour and that as music is embedded within this urban life, it is evident that it delineates time and place (Krims 2007, p. xviii). It is unlikely that grime music would have emerged from the leafy suburbs of Richmond-upon-Thames, because there is a symbiotic relationship between music, place and community, particularly as it relates to new musical practices that come out of movement and migration (Connell and Gibson 2003).

The east London area has a long history of movement and migration, from the French Huguenots who came to Spitalfields in the seventeenth century to Jewish settlement in the early twentieth century. This was followed by the subsequent migration from the Caribbean, Africa and the Indian subcontinent from the 1950s onwards (London Borough of Hackney 2005; London Borough of Newham 2005; London Borough of Tower Hamlets 2005; Tames 2006). Currently Newham and Tower Hamlets have higher populations of Asian and British Asian (34 per cent) than London as a whole, while Hackney's Black British population stands at 20.9 per cent (Neighbourhood Statistics 2007). Since the 1880s the Tower Hamlets areas of Limehouse and Stepney have also had a significant, but now declining, Chinese population (Benton and Gomez 2011). On the whole, east London has remained a multicultural, relatively poor part of London, despite its proximity to the city and local and national initiatives for regeneration. The *Thinkpiece Report*, prepared by MacRury and Poynter, was commissioned by the Communities and Local Government Department with a brief to identify socio-economic problems in the five host boroughs and map out a legacy for the London 2012 Olympic Games. It outlines the situation of east London as a site that had remained relatively poor since the nineteenth century, the impact of the closure of the docks and the subsequent regeneration intitiatives creating 'an area that is socially polarized, containing pockets of relative affluence within an area that has a high concentration of relative poverty and deprivation' (MacRury and Poynter 2009, p. 5).

Hackney was created as a metropolitan borough in 1899, formed out of the areas of Stoke Newington, Shoreditch and Hackney. The second half of the nineteenth century was characterised by rapid population growth. The current urban landscape was mainly created in the Victorian era with the railway arriving in 1840. In the 1930s the London County Council began a programme of slum clearance, and the building of the large housing estates stems from this era. After World War II, many industries began to move out of Hackney and Shoreditch. Margaret Thatcher's restructuring of the UK economy in the 1970s and 1980s led to the closure or relocation overseas of larger manufacturing firms. These firms were replaced by low-intensity enterprises such as car dealerships, scrap dealerships and cheap warehousing.

Five miles to the east of the City of London, and developing from a farming community in the mid-nineteenth century, Newham was formed from the old boroughs of East Ham and West Ham. The Royal Docks, built in the 1850s, linked directly to the railways. They were, at that time, one of the largest docks in the world and brought people from all over the world into east London. For example, in the 1930s Canning Town was home to the Coloured Men's Institute and at that time had the largest black population in London. Both the Docks and Newham experienced heavy bombing during the World War II, particularly in the south of the borough. West Ham developed small townships, including Canning Town and Silvertown, to house the workers for the new industries. In East Ham, the houses were built for professional workers, and so the two areas developed in different ways: West Ham was heavily industrialised, whereas East Ham – although it had Beckton Gasworks – had more open space, including Central Park, Plashet Park and Wanstead Flats (London Borough of Newham 2005).

Like Hackney, Newham experienced slum clearance and industrial decline, with high unemployment in the 1980s. In the last twenty years there have been significant regeneration initiatives. The London Docklands Development Corporation was formed in 1981 to regenerate Beckton and the Royal Docks, new housing was built in Beckton, including Cyprus, and London City Airport was built in 1987. Tower Hamlets has a similar history. Its development is most recently marked by the creation and development of Canary Wharf as a new fiscal location, with multinational companies such as HSBC and JP Morgan based there (FX Week 2003; Pratley 2010). All three boroughs were host boroughs for the London 2012 Olympics and are, post Games, currently undergoing another period of reconstruction and regeneration. In *Rebel Cities* (2013), David Harvey points out that in the social production of urban space, the creation of separate spaces and places has replaced integration – and it can be seen that places like Canary Wharf in Tower Hamlets and the Westfield Shopping centre in Newham create new spatial barriers between rich and poor. Nevertheless, place is a complex entity: it is contested and is continually in the process of becoming; it is not fixed. The production of place through music is therefore also a contested process, and there is a strong link with music and a sense of place (Hudson 2006).

Why entrepreneurship matters

Entrepreneurship, however it is defined, is seen as a significant factor for economic growth and all the more important as the developed world endeavours to pull itself out of an acute global recession. It is almost a given that individuals with entrepreneurial behaviours are vital for economic success. To this end, much research in this area has focused on the attributes, traits and behaviours that individuals are deemed to have. A manifestation of this is the current UK policy to develop entrepreneurship skills and attributes among young people through the implementation of enterprise education in primary and secondary schools (Schoof 2006; Ofsted 2011).

Entrepreneurship has been an area for scholarly inquiry since the 1980s (Baumol 1996; Blanchflower and Oswald 1998; Carland *et al.* 2002; Aldrich and Martinez 2001; Stevenson and Jarillo 1990). Definitions of the term reflect the focus on who entrepreneurs are and the impact of their activities. In classical economics to be an entrepreneur simply meant to be a 'businessman'. In the nineteenth century, J S Mill brought the term 'entrepreneur' into general use. Jean Baptiste Say extended the definition to include a person who brings together the factors of production. However, it appears that there is no unifying theme or conceptual framework regarding the question of what is an entrepreneur or indeed what is entrepreneurship (Gartner 1988), and it is often used in a very loose, generic sense (Gopakumar 1995; Shane and Venkataraman 2000). Some scholars argue that for the term to be of any use, the definition needs to be kept broad and include large organisations, management, start-ups, self-employment and small business (Cunningham and Lischeron 1991; Aldrich and Martinez 2001; Stevenson and Jarillo 1990).

Schumpeter expounded a concept focused on *creative destruction*, or the method by which an entrepreneur's drive for innovation leads to new ways of doing business either within or external to an organisation (Schumpeter 1994). This is an idea that is further developed by other researchers such as Carland, who point out that while there is overlap between entrepreneurs and small business owners – as both seek an innovative combination of resources for profit – it is possible and necessary to distinguish between the two because ownership is not a prerequisite for entrepreneurial behaviour (Carland *et al.* 1984). For Drucker, it is someone who seeks change and exploits the opportunity that that change brings about (Drucker 2006), and Baumol defines entrepreneurs as 'persons who are ingenious and creative in finding ways to add to their own power and prestige' (Baumol 1996, p. 897). Nevertheless, the Schumpeterian concept of innovation has been a key aspect of the study of entrepreneurs and entrepreneurship either through exploiting the value of new ideas or by carrying out new activities (McClelland 1967; Carland *et al.* 2002). This innovation can involve new products and services or the creation of a new organisation (Vesper 1980; Brockhaus Sr 1994). Shane and Venkataraman go further with this to suggest it is not just the creation of new organisations but the meeting of two crucial points: the presence of lucrative opportunities and the actions of enterprising individuals (Shane and Venkataraman 2000).

Nevertheless, as Williams points out, we are no nearer to coming up with an agreed definition for an entrepreneur or indeed for enterprise culture – 'you just know it when you see it' (Williams 2006, p. 16). For some researchers, however, this difficulty in creating a standard definition may be because, as a concept, it has no meaning and may be just an 'empty signifier' of a mythical being (Jones and Spicer 2005).

Existing research within this area has two main strands: first, at the individual level, looking at the motivations of the person; and second, explorations of organisations or structures that have been created. Stevenson and Jarillo add an additional category: how the actions of the entrepreneur impact on the economic system (Stevenson and Jarillo 1990). Research into the individual looks at what entrepreneurs actually do and tries to identify a common set of behaviours, for example having an internal locus of control, the need for independence and the drive to create wealth. McClelland's key text, *The Achieving Society*, looked at what constitutes an entrepreneurial personality (McClelland 1967). Behavioural, or trait, approaches attempt to understand psychological traits, attributes and socio-economic conditions and drivers of the individuals who provide entrepreneurship (Kets de Vries 1996; Baron 2000). Some scholars argue that researchers have so far failed to discover a cause-and-effect relationship between personality type/background and entrepreneurial success. This has added to the mythical status of entrepreneurs and the notion that they are not 'like us' as they have some unique characteristics that set them apart, such as their higher levels of social competence, and enable them to interact and adapt to new social situations more easily than others (Baron 2000; Johansson 2004).

Entrepreneurship is viewed as a process by which an economy as a whole can move forward. It disrupts the equilibrium of the market (through innovation and new combinations) and creates movement. It is therefore assumed to be at the root of economic improvement and the key to economic growth, productivity and the diffusion of knowledge. There is a correlation between the number of entrepreneurs and the growth rate of the economy; indeed, new firm creation is seen as a driving force for economic growth (Low and MacMillan 1988; Schumpeter 1994; Baumol 1996; Stevenson and Jarillo 1990). For Henderson and Weiler, entrepreneurship is crucial for long-term growth prospects because business creation can have 'significant impacts across space and time'. They outline the relationships between innovation, entrepreneurship and growth and find that entrepeneurship has its greatest impact in the region in which it occurs but also generates positive scope for job growth particularly in dense urban settings (Henderson and Weiler 2010). The impact of technology is changing the meaning of enterprise and entrepreneurial activity and it now occurs in everyday spaces and places and develops from commonplace activity (Peters and Besley 2008).

Conclusion

My research opens up a dialogue with participants in the urban music economy and relays what they are doing in their own words and actions. Against a backdrop of rising youth unemployment and increasing concern about disaffected youth, gangs and knife crime, the problem of the NEET becomes increasingly heightened. Music genres such as grime, created and disseminated within this context, are viewed as part of the problem. The reduction in the numbers of young people who become NEET therefore continues to be a priority, yet opportunities to partake in quality education and employment are limited in areas of advanced marginality such as the inner east London boroughs of Newham, Tower Hamlets and Hackney. Large numbers of young people leave full-time secondary education without the required five grade A*–C GCSEs for entry into further education. Grime music emerged out of these east London areas in the early twenty-first century. Grime and its related enterprise is a key component of the urban music economy. It has a local, national and global reach, and I now turn to the achievements of Dizzee Rascal, one of its best known protagonists, to lay the foundations for the remainder of the book.

References

Aldrich, H.E. and Martinez, M.A., 2001. Many are called, but few are chosen: An evolutionary perspective for the study of entrepreneurship. *Entrepreneurship Theory and Practice* 25(4), pp. 41–56.

Allen, M. and Ainley, P., 2007. *Education make you fick, innit?: What's gone wrong in England's schools, colleges and universities and how to start putting it right*, London, UK: Tufnell Press.

Ball, J., Milmo, D. and Ferguson, B., 2012. Half of UK's young black males are unemployed. *Guardian*. Available at: www.guardian.co.uk/society/2012/mar/09/half-uk-young-black-men-unemployed [accessed 12 April 2012].

Baron, R.A., 2000. Psychological perspectives on entrepreneurship. *Current Directions in Psychological Science*, 9(1), pp. 15–18.

Bassnett, S., 2007. What is education for? *openDemocracy*. Available at: www.open democracy.net/article/what_is_education_for [accessed 14 December 2013].

Baumol, W.J., 1996. Entrepreneurship: Productive, unproductive, and destructive. *Journal of Business Venturing*, 11(1), pp. 3–22.

Benn, M., 2012. *School wars: The battle for Britain's education*, London: Verso.

Benton, G. and Gomez, E.T., 2011. *Chinese in Britain, 1800-present*, Houndmills: Palgrave Macmillan.

Bingham, J., 2013. White boys 'the problem' for Britain's schools, says Government aide, Telegraph. Available at: www.telegraph.co.uk/education/educationnews/10375879/White-boys-the-problem-for-Britains-schools-says-Government-aide.html [accessed 19 October 2013].

Blanchflower, D.G. and Oswald, A.J., 1998. What makes an entrepreneur? *Journal of Labor Economics*, 16(1), pp. 26–60.

du Bois-Reymond, M., 2004. Youth – learning – Europe: Ménage à trois? *Young*, 12(3), pp. 187–204.

Brockhaus Sr, R.H., 1994. Entrepreneurship and family business research: Comparisons, critique, and lessons. *Entrepreneurship: Theory and Practice*, 19(1).

Campion, C., 2004. A look at grime music | Music | Observer Music Monthly. Available at: www.guardian.co.uk/music/2004/may/23/urban1 [accessed 13 April 2012].

Carland, J.W., Hoy, F., Boulton, W.R. and Carland, J.A. 1984. Differentiating entrepreneurs from small business owners: A conceptualisation. *Academy of Management Review* 9(2), pp. 354–359.

Carland, J.W., Hoy, F. and Carland, J.A., 2002. 'Who is an entrepreneur?' is a question worth asking. *Entrepreneurship: Critical perspectives on business and management*, p. 178.

Casson, M., 1979. *Youth unemployment*, New York: Holmes & Meier Publishers.

Connell, J. and Gibson, C., 2003. *Sound tracks: Popular music, identity, and place*, London and New York: Routledge.

Cunningham, J.B. and Lischeron, J., 1991. Defining entrepreneurship. *Journal of Small Business Management*, 29(1).

Curtis, P., 2008. Youth crime: Greedy, rude adults 'fuelling teen violence'. *Guardian*. Available at: www.theguardian.com/education/2008/jul/11/schools.uk [accessed 20 October 2013].

Department for Education, 2013. Ethnic minority achievement – Schools. Available at: www.education.gov.uk/schools/pupilsupport/inclusionandlearnersupport/mea/a0013246/ethnic-minority-achievement [accessed 20 October 2013].

Dreamers row, 2012. 10 years of grime: A genre that defined a generation. *Dreamers Row*. Available at: www.dreamersrow.com/10-years-of-grime-a-genre-that-defined-a-generation [accessed 21 June 2012].

Drucker, P.F., 2006. *Innovation and entrepreneurship*, London and New York: Harper-Collins.

Furlong, A. and Cartmel, F., 2007. *Young people and social change new perspectives*, Maidenhead: McGraw-Hill/Open University Press.

FX Week, 2003. HSBC relocates to Canary Wharf. *www.fxweek.com*. Available at: www.fxweek.com/fx-week/news/1535416/hsbc-relocates-canary-wharf [accessed 1 January 2014].

Gartner, W.B., 1988. Who is an entrepreneur? Is the wrong question. *American Journal of Small Business*, 12(4), pp. 11–32.

Gopakumar, K., 1995. The entrepreneur in economic thought: A thematic overview. *Journal of Entrepreneurship*, 4(1), pp. 1–17.

Hamnett, C., Ramsden, M. and Butler, T., 2007. Social background, ethnicity, school composition and educational attainment in East London. *Urban Studies*, 44(7), pp. 1255–1280.

Hampson, S., 2009. Interview: Geeneus – FACT magazine: Music and art. Available at: www.factmag.com/2009/01/01/interview-geeneus [accessed 11 September 2010].

Hancox, D., 2013. *Stand up tall: Dizzee Rascal and the birth of grime*, Kindle.

Harrison, A., 2013. One in 10 new graduates jobless. *BBC*. Available at: www.bbc.co.uk/news/education-23080323 [accessed 1 January 2014].

Harvey, D., 2013. *Rebel cities: From the right to the city to the urban revolution*, London and New York: Verso Books.

Henderson, J. and Weiler, S., 2010. Entrepreneurs and job growth: Probing the boundaries of time and space. *Economic Development Quarterly*, 24(1), pp. 23–32.

Hills, J., 2010. National equality panel. Available at: www.equalities.gov.uk/national_equality_panel.aspx [accessed 20 December 2010].

Hudson, R., 2006. Regions and place: Music, identity and place. *Progress in Human Geography*, 30(5), pp. 626–634.

Johansson, A.W., 2004. Narrating the entrepreneur. *International Small Business Journal*, 22(3), pp. 273–293.

Jones, C. and Spicer, A., 2005. The sublime object of entrepreneurship. *Organization*, 12(2), pp. 223–246.

journeymanpictures, 2008. *London Gangs – UK*, Available at: www.youtube.com/watch?v=4YH0LUt8R2k&feature=youtube_gdata_player [accessed 16 September 2010].

Kets de Vries, M.F.R., 1996. The anatomy of the entrepreneur: Clinical observations – Human relations. Available at: http://hum.sagepub.com/content/49/7/853.abstract [accessed 16 September 2010].

Kingsley, P., 2011. Despair and desperation – The real story of youth unemployment in Britain. *Guardian*. Available at: www.theguardian.com/society/2011/nov/01/despair-desperation-behind-youth-unemployment [accessed 22 September 2013].

Krims, A., 2007. *Music and urban geography*, New York: Routledge.

Lee, N. and Wright, J., 2011. *Off the map? The geography of NEETs: A snapshot analysis for the Private Equity Foundation*, Lancaster University: Work Foundation.

Leitch, L., 2006. Leitch review of skills: Prosperity for all in the global economy: World-class skills. *HM Treasury*.

London Borough of Hackney, 2005. Hackney local improvement plan.

London Borough of Newham, 2005. Newham local implementation plan.

London Borough of Tower Hamlets, 2005. Tower Hamlets local implementation plan. (2005).

Low, M.B. and MacMillan, I.C., 1988. Entrepreneurship: Past research and future challenges. *Journal of Management*, 14(2), pp. 139–161.

LSN, 2009. *Tackling the NEETs problem*, London: LSN.

MacDonald, R., 2011. Youth transitions, unemployment and underemployment: Plus ça change, plus c'est la même chose? *Journal of Sociology*, 47(4), pp. 427–444.

MacLeod, D., 2006. School leavers lack basic skills, say universities, *Guardian*. Available at: www.guardian.co.uk/education/2006/feb/09/highereducation.uk1 [accessed 20 December 2010].

MacRury, I. and Poynter, G., 2009. *London's Olympic legacy*, University of East London: London East Research Institute.

Mail Online, 2007. Four new arrests in Adam Regis murder hunt. *Mail Online*. Available at: www.dailymail.co.uk/news/article-443190/Four-new-arrests-Adam-Regis-murder-hunt.html [accessed 20 October 2013].

McClelland, D.C., 1967. *The achieving society*, New York: Free Press.

Murray, S. and Gayle, V., 2012. *Youth transitions*, University of Stirling.

Neighbourhood Statistics, 2007. Trend view. Available at: www.neighbourhood.statistics. gov.uk/dissemination/LeadTrendView [accessed 30 January 2011].

Office for National Statistics, 2013. *Full report: Graduates in the UK labour market 2013*, ONS.

Ofsted, 2011. *Economics, business and enterprise education*, Manchester, UK: Ofsted.

Panorama, 2009. 'We will come for you', gangs warned. *BBC*. Available at: http://news. bbc.co.uk/panorama/hi/front_page/newsid_8366000/8366280.stm [accessed 1 December 2010].

Peters, M.A. and Besley, T., 2008. Academic entrepreneurship and the creative economy. *Thesis Eleven*, 94(1), pp. 88–105.

Pratley, N., 2010. JP Morgan buys Lehman Brothers' former office in Canary Wharf. *Guardian*. Available at: www.theguardian.com/business/2010/dec/20/jp-morgan-lehman-brothers-hq [accessed 1 January 2014].

Ramesh, 2013. England's young people near bottom of global league table for basic skills. *Guardian*. Available at: www.theguardian.com/education/2013/oct/08/england-young-people-league-table-basic-skills-oecd [accessed 8 October 2013].

Richardson, B., 2007. *Tell it like it is: How our schools fail black children*, 2nd edn, Bookmarks.

Rose, A., 2008. Teenage knife and gun fatalities hit an all-time high. *Guardian*. Available at: www.guardian.co.uk/world/2008/dec/28/knife-crime-deaths-eyewitness [accessed 9 July 2012].

Scarman, L.S., Great Britain & Home Office, 1982. *The Brixton disorders, 10–12 April 1981: The Scarman report: Report of an inquiry*, Harmondsworth, Middlesex and New York: Penguin Books.

Schoof, U., 2006. *Stimulating youth entrepreneurship: Barriers and incentives to enterprise start-ups by young people*, Geneva: International Labour Office.

Schumpeter, J.A., 1994. *Capitalism, socialism and democracy*, Hove, UK: Psychology Press.

Sergeant, H., 2009a. Feral youths: How a generation of violent, illiterate young men are living outside the boundaries of civilised society, *Mail Online*. Available at: www.dailymail.co.uk [accessed 15 September 2010].

Sergeant, H., 2009b. *Wasted: The betrayal of white working class and black Caribbean boys*, London: Centre for Policy Studies.

Shane, S. and Venkataraman, S., 2000. The promise of entrepreneurship as a field of research. *Academy of Management Review* 25(1), pp. 217–226.

Shepherd, J., 2010. Poor literacy and maths skills leave teenagers ill-equipped, *Guardian*. Available at: www.guardian.co.uk/education/2010/may/07/poor-literacy-numeracy [accessed 20 December 2010].

Sherwin, A., 2007. Pirate radio DJs risk prosecution to fight gun and knife crime, *Times Online*. Available at: www.timesonline.co.uk/tol/news/uk/article2288801.ece [accessed 24 August 2011].

Sissons, P. and Jones, K., 2012. *Lost in transition? The changing labour market and young people not in employment, education or training*, London: Work Foundation.

Skidmore, C., 2008. Boys: A school report. *London: Bow Group*.

Stevenson, H.H. and Jarillo, J.C., 1990. A paradigm of entrepreneurship: Entrepreneurial management. *Strategic Management Journal* 11, pp. 17–27.

Stickler, A., 2008. Guns and knives on the streets. *BBC*. Available at: http://news.bbc.co.uk/today/hi/today/newsid_7773000/7773718.stm [accessed 20 October 2013].

Stone, J., 2016. All schools are to be forced to become academies whether parents like it or not. *Independent*. Available at: www.independent.co.uk/news/uk/politics/every-school-will-be-forced-to-become-an-academy-government-to-announce-a6932466.html [accessed 22 April 2016].

Tames, R., 2006. *London: A cultural history*, New York: Oxford University Press.

Taylor, A., 2013. Europe's youth unemployment crisis in one grim map. *Houston Chronicle*. Available at: www.chron.com/technology/businessinsider/article/Europe-s-Youth-Unemployment-Crisis-In-One-Grim-Map-4867740.php#src=fb [accessed 26 October 2013].

Tomlinson, S., 2005. *Education in a post-welfare society*, 2nd edn, Maidenhead, UK: Open University Press.

Vesper, K.H., 1980. *New venture strategies*, Englewood Cliffs, NJ: Prentice-Hall.

Williams, C.C., 2006. *The hidden enterprise culture: Entrepreneurship in the underground economy*, Cheltenham, UK and Northampton, MA: Edward Elgar Publishing.

1   Introduction

I help them get on with their dream and keep it moving forward. You can have a video camera and record at home but it doesn't look as fresh when it's on TV. As a make-up artist, I'm part of that team, I see the product come alive, so that's why I like doing music videos. You can look back over the years and see the progression...

(Gillian, 27 – make-up artist/stylist – interviewed in 2011)

Starting out

When 18-year-old Dizzee Rascal won the 2003 Mercury Music Prize, he described his lived experience of growing up on the council estates of Tower Hamlets. In a subsequent BBC interview he was quoted as saying: 'I come from nothing – I come from the underground, pirate radio stations, I come from the ground man' (BBC News 2003). The erstwhile Dylan Mills was, by his own admission, regularly excluded from most lessons at Langdon Park Community School in Poplar (BBC News 2003; London Borough of Tower Hamlets 2005). At the time, the mainstream music industry struggled to categorise his creative expression, erroneously settling for 'UK rapper'.

I want to use this event as my starting point. By saying that he is 'coming from nothing', Dizzee Rascal articulates an east London that is home to some of the poorest wards in the UK. It suggests that underachieving at school and becoming categorised as NEET (not in employment, education or training) is a rite of passage into adulthood for many young people from poor areas and that the informal 'underground' economy – including pirate radio stations – are a repository for young people producing and consuming what at that time was a music genre without a name: grime.

This book is concerned with the invisible entrepreneurs who participate in the urban music economy in east London. These entrepreneurs are invisible because, to borrow a concept from Loic Wacquant, they belong to a stigmatised community and, like the 18-year-old Dizzee Rascal, they are young, black and poor (Wacquant 2007). It is my claim that the NEET category disguises and obscures the real and continuing activities, achievements and accomplishments of those operating in the informal creative sector. Young people, who are or who have been NEET, are creating their own employment opportunities and, in many instances, creating work for others through their participation in the urban music economy. These activities remain unseen on the whole to policymakers responsible for reducing youth unemployment, but highly discernible in a mediated world. The data relating to young people who are NEET tell part of the story, as do the statistics relating to educational underachievement of young people from marginalised communities (see, for example, LSN 2009; Ball *et al.* 2012; Department for Education 2013a; Office for National Statistics 2013), but there is another aspect, largely unwritten, and it is that which is the focus of this book.

Being NEET: operating on the margins

Without the golden ticket of five GCSEs grade A*–C, the spectre of the NEET category looms large, particularly for those young people who live in impoverished areas. The ramifications in terms of life chances and social inclusion of becoming and remaining NEET are too significant to be ignored. Youth unemployment remains around the one million mark, but for young people from impoverished backgrounds moving between unemployment and low-paid, poor quality work or training schemes is not a novel situation. It is a long-term pattern that has been the lived experience for previous generations of older workers from poor areas (Shildrick *et al.* 2010). What has changed is that the low-paid work now available requires increasing levels of certification. Therefore those that do not acquire the necessary standard of qualification are more likely to operate on the margins of employment.

NEET has existed as a designator and as an outcome since the late 1990s, but it has gained momentum against a backdrop of rising youth unemployment and the impact of the global economic downturn that began in 2008. Estimates of those who fit the criteria vary between 10 per cent and 20 per cent (Lee and Wright 2011; Department for Education 2013; London's Poverty Profile 2013). In the report *Wasted*, Harriet Sergeant presents a common stereotype of the NEET: a detached, often criminal individual who is as far away as it is possible to be from the education and employment sphere (Sergeant 2009). As a category that emerged from the lexicon of the now defunct Careers Service, NEET was originally used to identify school leavers who were 'Status Zero', in other words, neither Status 1 – employed, nor Status 2 – in education, nor Status 3 – in training. This category was applied to approximately 20 per cent of school leavers in the mid 1990s (Shildrick *et al.* 2010).

Reducing the numbers of those who are classified as NEET has been a key youth policy for successive governments during the last fifteen years (LSN 2009; Shildrick *et al.* 2010; Lee and Wright 2011; Cunningham 2012). The New Labour government in 1997 pledged that it would increase young people's participation in work, education and training because the consequence of a lack of integration into formal work and adult life has a social impact, rising criminal and antisocial activity being one aspect of this. There is also, of course, a financial and economic burden, which is estimated in some quarters to be between

£12 and £32 billion. It includes the cost of paying for welfare benefits and increased instances of interactions with the criminal justice system (Coles *et al.* 2010). However it is defined, the NEET problem is an enduring socio-economic issue and one that the Conservative-led coalition government elected in 2010 maintained that it was firmly committed to tackling (HM Government 2011). The 2015 Conservative government continues the remit to reducing the number of young people who are NEET. However, their policy proposals effectively replace youth unemployment with unpaid work by introducing compulsory boot-camps or community work, removing housing benefit from 18–21 year olds and abolishing Jobseekers Allowance (JSA) for 18–21 year olds (Mason and Perraudin 2015).

Despite various policy interventions, in London the proportion of those who are NEET has not altered significantly over the last decade (Bainbridge and Browne 2010). The constituency that inhabits the NEET category is defined as static, immobile and restricted in terms of life chances and entry into the labour market (Bainbridge and Browne 2010). A variety of factors have been identified to determine those at risk of becoming NEET, but the most significant are being poor and unemployed, living in a poor neighbourhood, being from a particular ethnic minority background – specifically African Caribbean, Bangladeshi or Pakistani – and having few or no educational qualifications (Coles *et al.* 2010).

The east London boroughs of Newham, Tower Hamlets and Hackney are the starting point for this book. These boroughs contain areas that are high in socio-economic disadvantage, have some of the most ethnically diverse communities in the UK and have a high percentage of young people who are classified as NEET (London Borough of Newham 2005; London Borough of Hackney 2005; London Borough of Tower Hamlets 2005; Aston Mansfield 2011).

The urban music economy: context and definitions

Grime is a key component of the urban music economy. I am using 'urban' here to denote particular types of popular black musical expression such as grime, bassline, UK funky, garage, dubstep and RnB, but it is not an unproblematic category. For some the urban label is imposed on them by commerce and the media, who want to create neatly packaged and palatable versions of black musical expression. Indeed, there is a significant mismatch between perceptions of black culture by outsiders as 'cool' and the often harsh reality of being black and living on a deprived London council estate. In an interview in 2010, my informant Victor offered this vehement response to my question about his longevity in the urban music scene: 'Urban created a pothole for us ... urban means black and trouble ... urban events are shit, urban is a mental prison, it's a state of mind created to keep us in our place....'. According to the Oxford English Dictionary, 'urban' is defined as follows: 'in, relating to, or characteristic of a town or city: *the urban population* (also urban contemporary) denoting or relating to popular dance music of black origin: *hip-hop's traditionally urban vibe*'.

Over the last ten years the UK music industry appears to have embraced this term as a substitute or shorthand for the majority of black music genres. An example of this is the establishment of BBC Radio 1Xtra in 2002, with a brief to broadcast urban music, which it broadly defines as hip-hop, grime, bassline, garage, dubstep, RnB, drum and bass, UK funky, dancehall, reggae and Afrobeat. The Black Music Awards events (1992–1996) had the same musical constituency as the Music of Black Origin, or MOBO, awards (1996) and the Urban Music Awards (Urban Music Awards 2013). The debate surrounding the title of the MOBOs has abated. Since then, urban appears to be the standard nomenclature for certain kinds of music, namely, hip-hop, RnB, soul and grime.

It is nonetheless a problematic category, which Simon Wheatley alludes to in the title of his photographic grime project, *Don't Call Me Urban* (Wheatley 2010). At one level it is an inclusive label, enabling those who create or perform certain genres to be included; on the other, it is divisive. What of black musicians who create Rock music, for example, or artists such as Blur or Oasis, whose music is by definition 'relating to or characteristic of a town or city'? The furore when Joss Stone, a white soul singer from Devon, won best urban act in 2005 ahead of Dizzee Rascal, Lemar and Jamelia demonstrates the confusion and resistance that use of this term brings (BBC News 2005). Nevertheless, I have opted to use the term as a useful, albeit contested, shorthand for specific genres of black music.

Creative economy and the creative industries

The urban music economy forms part of the wider creative economy. In 2008, UNCTAD (United Nations Conference on Trade and Development) carried out the first global in-depth survey into the creative economy. This survey, and the subsequent report in 2010, suggest that creative industries are stimulating economic recovery and that the creative economy is a growing sector; for example, between 2002 and 2008 global exports of goods and services had an average growth rate of 14 per cent (UNCTAD 2010). Despite the fiscal downturn from 2008 to 2009 and the subsequent economic recession, the creative sector continued to grow (Newbigin 2010; CBI 2013). There is a clear link between the development of creative industries and economic growth and innovation (Flew 2011). The term 'creative industries' emerged as a response to the global economic restructuring, which has creativity at its core (Townley *et al.* 2009). Since the late 1990s, the creative industries have been viewed as a foundation for the post-industrial economy in the UK. The reasons for this include the significance of the cultural sectors for wealth creation, in that they have a key role to play in economic growth (CBI 2013). Nevertheless, it has been argued that as a category, 'creative industries' implies a commodification that does not recognise the non-monetary value of cultural and creative practice (Townley *et al.* 2009).

Although some authors agree that the creative industries produce social meaning in the form of texts and symbols, what constitutes creative and cultural industry is contested (Markusen *et al.* 2008). In the United Kingdom, the Department for Culture, Media and Sport (DCMS) recognises eleven creative sectors, including advertising, architecture, arts and antiques markets, crafts, design, fashion, film/video and photography, software, television and radio (DCMS 2010). Hesmondhalgh and Baker's definition of creative industries includes music recording and publishing (2011b). Furthermore, this list-based approach fails to take into account the technological convergence between sectors (Flew and Cunningham 2010; Townley *et al.* 2009). The Internet and digital media production are changing the relationship between producers and consumers. Media users are now able to work autonomously and, in what Yochai Benkler terms a 'social production model', create collaborative networks and peer production (Benkler 2006). In this model, media producers are generating new sources of competition.

Markusen *et al.* adopt an occupation and industry approach in their analysis of the creative economy, looking at what workers actually do and where their production is located. Using the research findings of *The New England Creative Economic Initiative* (NCEI) conducted in 1998, they use a broad definition for the creative economy to demonstrate that creative enterprise and individuals make a significant contribution to the regional and local economy. The NCEI also identified three components to the creative economy: creative clusters, comprising both enterprise and individuals directly and indirectly creating cultural products; a creative workforce (people trained in specific cultural and artistic skills); and a creative community (a geographical area with a concentration of creative workers, creative businesses and cultural organisations) (Markusen *et al.* 2008, p. 30). For Peters and Besley, drawing on Schumpeter's concept of creative destruction, a creative economy is one where ideas rather than land or capital are the key components (Peters and Besley 2008, p. 89).

Conceptual framework

The organising framework for this book is Paul Gilroy's concept of the black Atlantic, particularly as it relates to the transnational and borderless flow of black creative expression (Gilroy 1996). The black Atlantic concept is a heuristic device that challenges notions of nationality, authenticity and cultural integrity and allows for an analysis of the hybrid forms of creative expression produced predominantly by those from the black diaspora. These hybrid cultural forms draw on the Caribbean, America and Africa and have been reworked for and in Britain. Within this context, cultural expression does not flow in line within national borders; instead, it moves back and forth, crossing boundaries and changing shape. It provides a way to analyse transnational and intercultural flow of creative expression. This analysis has a global significance, because it can be used to explore the remaking of ethnic identities. For black Britons, an intermixture of distinct cultural forms has enabled the creation of a compound culture from disparate sources. New black vernacular creative expression and hybridised identities have been created from this intermixture.

The black Atlantic trope is therefore used to explore the origins, location and flow of grime music. Grime is then used as a lens to examine and analyse the NEET category, because this music genre and its related business activity are a cornerstone of the urban music economy. Its origins, practice and dissemination lie with the black Atlantic construct.

In poor inner-city areas, such as the London boroughs of Tower Hamlets, Newham and Hackney, which are the geographical starting point for this book, people seek out opportunities in the informal sector as an alternative or a supplement to 'poverty wages with no benefits' (Wacquant 2007, p. 66). Because the practitioners in this sector appear to belong to ethnically stigmatised communities, I draw on the work of Loïc Wacquant to consider whether the concept of 'advanced marginality' impacts participation in the informal creative economy.

Wacquant's insistence that the debate regarding inequality and marginality be situated in the dismantling of post Fordist-Keynesian economics and the intersection of poverty, racial division and post-colonial immigration is especially useful to my analysis of the urban music economy. Poor neighbourhoods are often sites of advanced marginality with wage labour as a source of social fragmentation, particularly for those at the borders, for example those on temporary or zero-hours contracts. In these areas there is a disconnect from global economic trends, in that the conditions for the poor stay the same whatever happens in the world. In reality, social mobility and material conditions change very little. Advanced marginality also means the creation of 'isolated and bounded territories' perceived by both insiders and outsiders as badlands where only 'the refuse of society would agree to dwell', therefore special measures can be used by the state to manage and control these 'lawless zones' (Wacquant 2007, pp. 236–237). In the post-Fordist economic era, the east London boroughs of Hackney, Tower Hamlets and Newham have lost local jobs and become disconnected from traditional mechanisms of mobility such as educational achievement (Blanden and Machin 2007; Rogers 2012). As workers, this community has been made expendable by advances in technology. Some of the highest numbers of workless households in London can be found in these boroughs (London Councils 2010, p. 42).

In this book I draw on the work of Michel Foucault to make my argument that in relation to the creative practice of artist-entrepreneurs in the urban music economy, disciplinary techniques of power and procedures of knowledge are used to impose order and create different kinds of space (Foucault 1991). These techniques involve the control of the body at an individual level, it is both incremental and specific and involves the supervision of the smallest detail. Discipline comes from the distribution of individuals in space. The techniques that enable this include enclosure, the physical confinement of the body using structures such as schools, military barracks and factories, which neutralises unmonitored individuals. Another technique is partitioning – each individual has his own place and vice versa, therefore groups and gatherings can be broken up, for the express purpose of knowing where people are, who is present and who is absent. This functional coding of architectural space can entail the offer of a service – employment or housing, perhaps – and supports the creation of the need for detailed recording and noting down. In other words, these techniques exist to pin down and partition the individual (Foucault 1991, p. 144). In the last decade, technology such as the camera phone has become more affordable and accessible, and YouTube and MySpace provide a relatively free space for broadcast and distribution of creative output. However, this rapid increase in accessible broadcasting opportunities also provides the means for further surveillance and regulation of marginalised groups.

A further disciplinary technique was the post-World War II slum clearance and the subsequent creation of local authority-owned housing estates. A segmentation of architectural space occurred as poorly regulated private housing provision gave way to the careful bureaucracy of the municipal housing department. The high unemployment of the post-Thatcher years had an enduring negative impact on working-class communities such as those in inner-city east London. There were deepening divisions between those that became part of the property-owning democracy by buying their council property, moving up the social ladder and then moving out of these areas of urban decline. Now, a residual working class remains in situ with little access to employment and intense competition for resources such as housing (MacRury and Poynter 2009). The shared outside spaces of these housing estates provided an opportunity for the young, white working class and the offspring of Commonwealth migrants to socialise and congregate, allowing for a flow and mix of creative expression.

All social life is essentially practical, and it is possible to construct a theoretical model of social practice by looking at aspects of everyday life within the urban music economy. An exploration of the grime music scene and its related enterprise allows for an analysis of how people start to get a sense of the limits and boundaries of their circumstances. Despite regeneration, including that of the London 2012 Olympics, particular pockets of east London continue to be sites of poverty and deprivation (London Borough of Hackney 2005; London Borough of Newham 2005; London Borough of Tower Hamlets 2005; MacRury and Poynter 2009). To this end Pierre Bourdieu's conceptualisation of social, economic and cultural capital is generative for grasping how the participants in the urban music economy produce creative objects and what value is placed on those creative objects.

High art such as opera, theatre and ballet does not, on the whole, operate within the informal urban music economy. Taste for the production and consumption of this type of creative expression lies with an elite minority who can set themselves apart from the masses. These creative pursuits are preserved, nurtured and funded by the state; for example, the Arts Council funds 47 per cent of the English National Opera's costs and provides £6 million for the upkeep of the English National Ballet (Arts Council 2013). Grime music, and those who produce it, comes out of inner-city east London. It therefore has little intrinsic value and, like other working-class creative practice, is assumed to have 'values which cheapen, degrade and even brutalise the sensibilities of the masses'

(Willis 2006, p. 569). The contradiction is that grime is also eagerly consumed by middle-class youth (Mason 2008; Hancox 2009). This formal arts establishment excludes the majority of young people and ignores or spurns the 'symbolic creativity' in everyday life, where a dynamic creative practice exists (Willis 2006).

The arts establishment supports the idea of the artist in the high art sector who holds a unique position creating fine works that resist the pull of mass consumerism. On the other hand, it appears that those operating in the urban music sector have a more practical relationship with commerce. Although Willis contends disadvantaged groups may want to use their creative activity to bypass formal recognition, there does appear to be a drive for visibility and recognition for participants in the urban music economy (Willis 2006).

In the quote that opens the chapter, Gillian talks about being able to 'look back over the years and see the progression'. This book considers how the urban music economy has evolved over the last decade and the progress, or otherwise, of the individuals in the sector as they strive to disseminate their creative practice and to make a living.

How the book is organised

This book draws on ethnographic field research carried out in the UK and Cyprus. To preserve the anonymity of the respondents, I have used pseudonyms. Biographical details are kept to a minimum. In Appendix 1, I provide a brief summary of the respondent's details as well as a more detailed breakdown of location, ethnic/cultural background and qualifications. Appendix 2 contains a reflection on the ethnographic process and outlines, in some depth, how the research was conducted. Appendix 2 also provides a schedule of interviews and other research activities. Chapter 2 (Grime in the city: kinship and belonging) outlines the history of grime and connects its sonic origins to Jamaican sound systems, hip-hop and RnB – reworked for the enclosed stairwells and tower blocks of east London. The social and economic significance of the grime music scene, both locally and globally, is outlined. It considers how enterprise is formulated as a resistance to attempts to pin down the grime scene. Because collaboration and conviviality are intrinsic to grime music production and to the wider urban music economy, these aspects are examined. Finally, the lived experience of intergenerational and peer-to-peer musical heritage among the practitioners is also explored. Part II looks at creative enterprise as social practice. Chapter 3 (Artist-entrepreneurs: working for love and money) explores the social and economic context of my informants. I consider the contradictions that arise from living in 'the ends' – toughened environments that act as sites of repressive practice as well as of comfort and security. In this chapter, I include direct dialogue with artist-entrepreneurs and report back on ethnographic research from four east London sites. Chapter 4 (Business studies from 'the ends': learning the rules of the game) explores the urban music economy in closer detail, locating it within the informal and formal economy. What is it that influences a young person to become an artist-entrepreneur in the urban music economy? Drawing on field research in the UK, I analyse how young people without formal qualifications and with access to meagre economic capital become artist-entrepreneurs and learn the rules of the game. In Chapter 5 (Enterprise abroad), I provide a case study from Ayia Napa on how a market has been created for urban music in Europe. I also explore, and provide evidence of, the mutual dependence of the formal and informal economy in this sector. In Chapter 6 (Crossing borders, moving on: the urban music economy as a transformative realm), I analyse the impact of declining social mobility over the last two decades. As a significant economic sector in the UK, the creative and cultural industries remain, for the most part, closed to young people from poor areas. It is within this context that the urban music economy is posited as a transformative realm, where new identities can be created. Many practitioners metamorphose into commercial 'brands' to pursue their dreams of making a living; therefore I also discuss and explore the neo-liberal agenda. Finally, in Chapter 7 (The wrap-up: entrepreneurship in the urban music economy) I pull together the key themes that permeate the book: how the NEET identification obscures the achievements of young people from poor areas, how practitioners in the grime music scene disrupt this category, and the social, economic and cultural importance of the urban music sector and its related enterprise activity.

References

Arts Council, 2013. Funding. Available at: www.artscouncil.org.uk/funding/ [accessed 14 December 2013].

Aston Mansfield, 2011. *Newham: Key statistics*, London: Aston Mansfield Charity.

Bainbridge, L. and Browne, A., 2010. *Generation Neet*, York: Report for Children and Young People Now Magazine.

Ball, J., Milmo, D. and Ferguson, B., 2012. Half of UK's young black males are unemployed. *Guardian*. Available at: www.guardian.co.uk/society/2012/mar/09/half-uk-young-black-men-unemployed [accessed 12 April 2012].

BBC News, 2003. Rapper Rascal wins Mercury Prize. *BBC*. Available at: http://news.bbc.co.uk/1/hi/entertainment/music/3092520.stm [accessed 11 September 2010].

BBC News, 2005. Brits debate over 'urban' music. *BBC*. Available at: http://news.bbc.co.uk/1/hi/entertainment/4253845.stm [accessed 1 February 2014].

Benkler, Y., 2006. *The wealth of networks: How social production transforms markets and freedom*, New Haven, CT: Yale University Press.

Blanden, J. and Machin, S., 2007. *Recent changes in intergenerational mobility in Britain*, London: Sutton Trust.

CBI, 2013. CBI: Creative industries: One of the fastest growing sectors in the UK. Available at: www.cbi.org.uk/business-issues/creative-industries [accessed 22 June 2013].

Coles, B., Godfrey, C., Keung, A., Parrott, S. and Bradshaw, J., 2010. *Estimating the lifetime cost of NEET: 16–18 year olds not in education, employment or training*, York: University of York.

Cunningham, A., 2012. NEETs: A lost generation. *Total Politics*. Available at: www.totalpolitics.com/articles/344172/neets-a-lost-generation.thtml [accessed 26 January 2013].

DCMS, 2010. Department for Culture Media and Sport: Creative industries. Available at: www.culture.gov.uk/what_we_do/creative_industries/default.aspx [accessed 20 December 2010].

Department for Education, 2013a. Ethnic minority achievement: Schools. Available at: www.education.gov.uk/schools/pupilsupport/inclusionandlearnersupport/mea/a0013246/ethnic-minority-achievement [accessed 20 October 2013].

Department for Education, 2013b. *NEET statistics quarterly brief: April to June 2013*, Department for Education. Available at: www.gov.uk/government/publications/neet-statistics-quarterly-brief-april-to-june-2013 [accessed 22 August 2013].

Flew, T., 2011. *The creative industries: Culture and policy*, London: Sage Publications.

Flew, T. and Cunningham, S.D., 2010. Creative industries after the first decade of debate. *The Information Society* 26(2), pp. 113–123.

Foucault, M., 1991. *Discipline and punish: The birth of the prison*, London: Penguin.

Gilroy, P., 1996. *The Black Atlantic*, London: Verso.

Hancox, D., 2009. 2009: The year grime began to pay. *Guardian*. Available at: www.theguardian.com/music/2009/dec/31/grime-2009-dizzee-rascal-tynchy-stryder [accessed 16 November 2013].

Hesmondhalgh, D. and Baker, S., 2011. *Creative labour: Media work in three cultural industries*, London and New York: Routledge.

HM Government, 2011. *Supporting youth employment: An overview of the coalition government's approach*, Prime Minister's Office.

Lee, N. and Wright, J., 2011. *Off the map? The geography of NEETs: A snapshot analysis for the Private Equity Foundation*, Lancaster University: Work Foundation.

London Borough of Hackney, 2005. Hackney local improvement plan.

London Borough of Newham, 2005. Newham local implementation plan.

London Borough of Tower Hamlets, 2005. Tower Hamlets local implementation plan.

London Councils, 2010. *Counting the cost: A worklessness costs audit for London*.

London's Poverty Profile, 2013. Not in education employment or training – 'NEETs' | Poverty Indicators | London's Poverty Report. Available at: www.londonspovertyprofile.org.uk/indicators/topics/low-educational-outcomes/not-in-education-employment-or-training--neets/ [accessed 28 September 2013].

LSN, 2009. *Tackling the NEETs problem*, London: LSN.

MacRury, I. and Poynter, G., 2009. *London's Olympic legacy*, University of East London: London East Research Institute.

Markusen, A., Wassall, G., DeNatale, D. and Cohen, R. 2008. Defining the creative economy: Industry and occupational approaches. *Economic Development Quarterly* 22(1), pp. 24–45.

Mason, M., 2008. *The pirate's dilemma: How hackers, punk capitalists, graffiti millionaires and other youth movements are remixing our culture and changing our world*, London: Penguin.

Mason, R. and Perraudin, F., 2015. Unemployed young people will be sent to work boot camp, says minister. *Guardian*. Available at: www.theguardian.com/society/2015/aug/17/unemployed-young-people-work-boot-camp-tory-minister [accessed 12 March 2016].

Newbigin, J., 2010. *The creative economy: An introductory guide*, London: British Council.

Office for National Statistics, 2013. Young people not in education, employment or training. *Office for National Statistics*. Available at: www.ons.gov.uk/ons/rel/lms/young-people-not-in-education-employment-or-training-neets-/august-2013/index.html [accessed 28 September 2013].

Peters, M.A. and Besley, T., 2008. Academic entrepreneurship and the creative economy. *Thesis Eleven*, 94(1), pp. 88–105.

Rogers, S., 2012. Social mobility: The charts that shame Britain, *Guardian*. Available at: www.theguardian.com/news/datablog/2012/may/22/social-mobility-data-charts [accessed 29 October 2013].

Sergeant, H., 2009. *Wasted: The betrayal of white working class and black Caribbean boys*, London: Centre for Policy Studies.

Shildrick, T., Macdonald, R., Webster, C. and Garthwaite, K., 2010. *The low-pay, no-pay cycle: Understanding recurrent poverty*, York, UK: Joseph Rowntree Foundation.

Townley, B., Beech, N. and McKinlay, A., 2009. Managing in the creative industries: Managing the motley crew. *Human Relations*, 62(7), pp. 939–962.

UNCTAD, 2010. Creative Economy Report 2010.

Urban Music Awards, 2013. About Us – Urban Music Awards. Available at: http://urban musicawards.net/about-us/ [accessed 4 February 2014].

Wacquant, L., 2007. *Urban outcasts: A comparative sociology of advanced marginality*, Cambridge, UK: Polity.

Wheatley, S., 2010. *Don't call me urban: The time of grime*, Newcastle-upon-Tyne: Northumbria University Press.

Willis, P., 2006. Symbolic creativity. In *Cultural theory and popular culture: A reader*. Athens, GA: University of Georgia Press, p. 657.

2 Grime in the city

Kinship and belonging

Well, I started off with jungle, moved on to garage and then it was the grime thing but everything goes back, at some stage, so I've gone back a bit. I play a bit of grime, play a bit of funky house, play old-school garage, a bit of reggae, everything really.

(Ian, 22 – club and radio DJ – interviewed in 2009)

Introduction

Grime music belongs to the city, but its sonic origins and influences, hip-hop, RnB, reggae and the cultural practice of Jamaican sound systems, flow through and are embedded within the black diaspora. The starting point for this book is urban east London, from where grime emerged in the opening years of the new millennium. As a black Atlantic creative expression that reaches beyond national borders, grime's most well-known exponent is arguably Dizzee Rascal. In this chapter, I look back over a decade of grime to argue that the space where Dizzee Rascal learned and then honed his craft lies within the broader picture of the movement and migration that encapsulates the east end of London and, on a smaller scale, the grime crew and the clandestine, claustrophobic setting of pirate radio. The crew is underpinned by friendship and kinship connections that allow for the creation of a landscape where young people, with limited resources, are able to create a thoroughly English black creative expression.

The early adoption of emerging technology by practitioners in this field means that social media, video sharing websites such as YouTube, and online TV channels have now superseded pirate radio for the dissemination of grime. However, although they are viewed as a threat to public safety, pirate radio stations afforded a unique opportunity for DJs and MCs to perform in public.

I contend that the grime music scene allows for a creative practice, nourished by familial influences, that articulates the here and now while reaching back into past cultural heritage. In this sector, young people work across boundaries and in collaboration, simultaneously occupying discrete and compound roles. A further connection to the operation of the Jamaican sound system is in the way that grime artists draw on this practice by utilising the enterprise element, thereby presenting a way to make a living through the sale of music and its related merchandise. As Ian states in the quote that opens this chapter, 'everything goes back, at some stage', so I now turn to a history of grime to bring us into the present.

Calling the past into the present: sound systems and a decade of grime

Long before rap was the CNN for the ghetto (D and Jah, 1997),[1] reggae music articulated the struggles of the poor in a newly independent Jamaica. In Jamaica, reggae could be heard via the sound systems, portable endeavours comprised of equipment (speakers, turntables, generator) and crew, particularly the selector – who assesses the vibe and chooses the records to suit – and the DJ – who 'toasts' or chats over the selected tunes. The sonic genealogy of grime can be traced back to these Jamaican sound systems, and this heritage is manifest in three key ways: first, through the role of the crew and contemporary examples such as Roll Deep, Pay as U Go, Heartless Crew and N.A.S.T.Y crew; second, through the 'sound clash' or adversarial performance battle; and finally, through grime MCs 'spitting' lyrics over a beat.

Grime has its origins in the hybridity genre of reggae, which itself grew out of a mix of North American and Caribbean musical forms. As a black Atlantic creative expression (Gilroy 1996),[2] its provenance is firmly rooted in urban east London, specifically the London boroughs of Tower Hamlets and Newham. Grime can be traced to a specific location, namely urban east London. It comes out of an inner-city environment where the offspring of Caribbean migrants intermingle with a white working-class population, and its linguistic canon reflects this. This genre has been created out of what Paul Gilroy calls the '… displacement, relocation and dissemination of black creative expression' (Gilroy 1996, p. 80). The practitioners in this field are predominantly, but not exclusively, young black males. Its consumers, however, are from all over the UK, Europe and, increasingly, Africa and North America.

When Dizzee Rascal, a grime MC – aka Dylan Mills – won the Mercury Music Prize in 2003, he described growing up in the east London area of Bow in an environment that consisted of the council estates of Tower Hamlets and regular exclusions from both classroom and school (BBC News Channel 2003b; London Borough of Tower Hamlets 2005). The inner east London area that Dizzee refers to has a long history of movement and migration, from the arrival of the French Huguenots who came to Spitalfields in the seventeenth century to the Jewish settlement of the early twentieth century. From the 1950s there was a steady flow of migration from the Commonwealth, specifically from the Caribbean, Africa and the Indian subcontinent (London Borough of Hackney 2005; London Borough of Newham 2005; London Borough of Tower Hamlets 2005; Tames 2006). Currently Newham and Tower Hamlets have higher populations of Asian and British Asian (34 per cent) than does London as a whole, while Hackney's Black British population stands at 20.9 per cent (Neighbourhood Statistics 2007). Since the 1880s the Tower Hamlets areas of Limehouse and

Stepney have also had a significant, but now declining, Chinese population (Benton and Gomez 2011). On the whole, east London has remained a multicultural, relatively poor part of London, despite its closeness to the city and local and national initiatives for regeneration – including the London 2012 Olympics.

Dizzee Rascal learned his craft via a sporadic apprenticeship with Roll Deep, where he was championed by the 'Godfather of Grime', Wiley, aka Richard Cowie, until artistic differences led to a parting of the ways.[3] Wiley and Dizzee lived within a few miles of each other, and Wiley was a founding member of Roll Deep, a grime crew of approximately a dozen young men from the inner east London borough of Tower Hamlets. Roll Deep included MCs Scratchy (Ryan Williams), Flow Dan (Mark Vieira), Riko Dan (Zane Williams), Trim (Javan St. Prix), Breeze, Jet Li, Bubbles, Pit Bull, Jamakabi and Tinchy Stryder (Kwasi Danquah), as well as DJs Karnage and Maximum and beatmaker Danny Weed (Daniel Baker). Target (Darren Joseph), initially a producer for Roll Deep, is now a DJ on BBC Radio 1Xtra. Tinchy Stryder has achieved national chart success.[4] In a recent interview, Danny Weed and Target reflected on their early grime days and discussed how they – along with Scratchy and Breeze – grew up together, with all of them at one point or another working in Wiley's dad's patty shop in east London. According to Danny Weed: 'We got free patties and shit money' (i-D Staff 2015). While the output from individual members has been intermittent of late, Roll Deep, including Wiley, signed to a major label and enjoyed national chart success.

Slightly further east in the London Borough of Newham, Marcus Nasty, aka Marcus Ramsay, Jammer (Jahmek Power) and other members of the N.A.S.T.Y crew were also formulating a new sound from the waning UK garage genre. N.A.S.T.Y, an acronym for Natural Artistic Sounds Touching You, was founded at the turn of the twenty-first century by Marcus Nasty, D Double E (Darren Dixon) and Jammer, until an acrimonious split left Marcus Nasty at the helm for a while. Like Roll Deep, this crew is also a fluid collection of approximately a dozen young male artists. Members included DJ Mak 10 (Nathaniel Ramsay) and MCs Griminal (Joshua Ramsay), Hyper, Stormin, Lil Nasty (Theo Ramsay), Ghetts (Justin Clarke), Sharky Major (Jerome Palmer) and Kano (Kane Robinson). In the early days, Dizzee Rascal worked with particular members of N.A.S.T.Y. crew. After the split, D Double E, Jammer and Footsie (Daniel Carnegie) transformed themselves into the Newham Generals and eventually signed to Dizzee Rascal's Dirtee Stank label. While N.A.S.T.Y. is no longer a prime force as a crew, the universally lauded pirate radio sets such as the 2002 clash, where they go back-to-back with Roll Deep, are legendary (British Grime/ Garage Music History 2013). Former members have evolved into different roles and genres: Marcus Nasty is a DJ on Rinse FM; Ghetts is an independent recording artist; Stormin is a drum and bass MC; and Jammer's Lord of the Mics (LOTM) annual MC clash is now in its tenth year.

A key component of both the sound systems and the subsequent UK garage and grime scene was, and is, the crew. In the urban music sector a crew is a group of like-minded individuals who are friends or have some kind of kinship connection and share a common interest, in this case music. So, for example So Solid, Heartless Crew, Boy Better Know (BBK), Pay As You Go, Roll Deep and N.A.S.T.Y crew have members who attended the same schools, grew up on the same estates, are brothers or have some kind of familial relationship. Music crew membership is concerned with an expression and performance firmly rooted in the black diaspora experience. Predominantly male, a crew is a space that provides an opportunity to learn your craft and develop tacit knowledge about the scene and how it operates. In the crew, roles and responsibilities are delineated and can comprise beatmakers, MCs, vocalists and producers, but members can and do cross boundaries, often moving temporarily or permanently between one role and another. However, I am drawing a clear distinction here between a 'gang', which may or may not have 'crew' in its name, and a crew in the context of urban music. A gang is seen to have come together for other activities and usually nefarious purposes. The primary purpose of the crew in this context is the creation, production and dissemination of music.

The grime scene offered a liminal space for young men from impoverished backgrounds with limited resources to create music that spoke to and of their surroundings – the street corners and council estates of east London – but that reached back into their Caribbean heritage. *Ina de Ghetto*, a grime track by Wretch 32 featuring Badness and Ghetts (formerly, Ghetto), demonstrates this and also speaks to a collision/collapse of space, time and place. The words are spoken and sung by the three artists in a London and Jamaican dialect, and some very lyrical wordplay is used to describe those who are focused on criminality as a way out of the hard life. The lyrics and visuals make connections between east London and Kingston; Jamaica, and illustrate how grime emerged from east London but draws on a distinctly Caribbean heritage to speak to a global audience.

At the age of sixteen, DJ Geeneus (Gordon Warren) founded Rinse FM (a former pirate radio station) in Tower Hamlets with DJ Slimzee. According to Geeneus, it was on Rinse FM in 2002 where UK garage began to evolve into grime: 'it was more like a darker side of garage. We kind of converted the scene, into a darker sound.... Grime started in east London' (Hampson 2009). Grime had indeed emerged from UK garage in the late twentieth and early twenty-first centuries. The garage scene, however, had been dogged by violence, sometimes fuelled by postcode affiliations, and soon what had started as an innovative UK take on US house music became a highly marginalised practice with very limited opportunities for artists to perform. As a result, South London garage crew So Solid found themselves in the curious position of having had national chart success but being unable to play live in London. In an interview in 2003, So Solid's MC Harvey said: 'if you had Westlife in here you'd ask about the album, but people ask us about the violence' (So Solid Crew 2006).

In the UK, particularly in London, shootings and stabbings at garage music events were reported with heightened media anxiety. Politicians opined on how this music, particularly the lyrical content, encouraged brutality and gang membership. The regulating authorities – police and local councils – waged war on a scene that they felt encouraged criminality (First Sight 2002; BBC News Channel 2003a; Plunkett 2003). Eventually, public performance of UK garage music became so problematic that it disappeared from view (Jackson 2005). The 'bling bling', or ostentatious, themes of garage reflected in tracks such as *Champagne Dance* gave way to a grittier oeuvre. In London the distinction between garage and what took its place hinged in part on postcodes, and north/south/east affiliations. South of the River Thames, as garage faded away, UK rap took its place, with the slower more laconic style typified by artists such as Giggs.

Grime is predominantly young, male and black. An arrhythmic, unconventional genre, it samples an eclectic mix of sounds structured around 140 bpm. It can be hard on the ear, the beats can be disturbing and brutal and sometimes, in the rapid-fire delivery, the words are almost imperceptible. Grime is, however, a means to express individuality in a public or community arena and a space where creative practice and commerce come together and enable the sale of black creative expression in a national and global marketplace (Hill Collins 2006). These artistic and entrepreneurial endeavours can take the form of live performance, the staging of events, the production and sale of mixtapes and other merchandise such as clothing and DVDs, the sale of studio time and the creation and distribution of publicity and marketing materials. At its heart are MCs, DJs, producers, beatmakers and promoters, almost all of them male. The female presence in this sector is a relatively small constituency. Shystie (Chanelle Scott Calica) is an MC from Hackney who has been performing for over a decade. She offered an early, spirited response to Dizzee Rascal's *I Luv U* in 2003. More recent entrants to the field include MC Lady Leshurr (Melesha O'Garro), actress and MC Paigey Cakey (Paige Meade) and Birmingham MC RoXXXan (Roxanne Conway).

In its formative years, grime used its own distinct marketing routes – radio, record shops and raves. Over a fourteen-year period, pirate radio station Rinse FM broadcast from a number of different tower blocks on various council estates. With Déjà Vu and Freeze, Rinse FM had a central role in showcasing grime. Before the Internet, independent record shops such as Rhythm Division provided products and information; meanwhile, regular club events such as Sidewinder and Eskimo Dance were an opportunity for artists to perform. In the early internet era, the diffusion of grime was supplemented by the social networking sites MySpace and Facebook and by digital TV, specifically Channel U[5] and YouTube (at the time a fledgling video sharing channel). As new platforms emerge – Twitter, Soundcloud, Instagram and Snapchat, for example – they form part of the everyday promotional tools for artists in this sector. The pirate radio network Channel AKA and YouTube form an influential and integral part of marketing and promoting urban music of all kinds, including grime. These avenues of promotion and distribution have been made possible by advances in technology. Participation in this arena therefore requires technological skill, collaborative activity and the exchange or barter of goods and services.

As a genre, grime has been cited as an incitement to gang membership, criminal activity and violence, particularly among young black men in inner-city

London and in other cities, such as Birmingham (Beauman 2006; Jones 2010; Muggs 2010). Simon Wheatley, who spent ten years photographing and curating the grime scene for his book *Don't Call Me Urban!*, agrees that there is a connection between the violence of the lyrics and the activities of the practitioners. However, in *Stand Up Tall*, Dan Hancox discusses the birth of grime and argues that

> while New Labour were flooding urban Britain with ASBOs and CCTV, teenagers like Dizzee looked up at the gleaming towers of Canary Wharf and contemplated their own poverty; telling stories of devastating bleakness, backed by music that shone with the futurism of a brighter tomorrow.
>
> (Hancox *et al.* 2013)

The significance and impact of grime as a genre lies somewhere within these two positions, a creative output that metaphorically, and sometimes literally, gives expression to life at the margins as an urban outcast while offering an opportunity for getting on by staying put or, indeed, for exit.

Like lovers' rock in the 1970s – a UK-specific reggae genre created by the offspring of Caribbean migrants to the UK – grime draws on the cultural, political and economic history of having parents and grandparents from elsewhere. It stakes a claim to the lived experience of a specific and particular place, in this case urban east London. It is an opportunity for artists to bring forth a character with which to tell stories from a fictional 'personal perspective' (Rose 1994). Asserting black urban identities rooted in, for example, Newham rather than Africa or the Caribbean, personas reflect the gritty nature of the environment, with a nomenclature that comprises weaponry (Klashnekoff, Mak 10), heat (Scorcher, Lightning), characteristics (Wiley, Slimzee, Trim, Brutal, Bruza) and lyrical wordplay (JME, for Jamie, Griminal, commit grime not crime). In a highly mediated sector, these personas constitute a positive act of creating a speaking subject; the masks are not an attempt to conceal identity. Within a context of marginalisation and silence, these stories are communicated through the musical performance and cover an array of motifs, including success or perceived success, the making of money, the originality of lyrics, and so on. But the themes also include friendship, teamwork, love, crime and visibility. The use of street vernacular within this genre is sovereign and it enables an oral passing on of biographies, stories and knowledge.

The foundations of grime music lie in, and are grounded in, the sound systems, shebeens and blues dances of the previous decades. In Jamaica in the 1950s, sound systems had started out playing American R n B imports, but in time this gave way to ska, followed by rocksteady and, ultimately, reggae. In the 1970s and 1980s each area of London and every big city with a black community of Caribbean heritage had a sound system.[6] Dancehall, a faster, sparser version of reggae, came to the fore in the late 1970s. By the mid 1980s, Wayne Smith's *Under Mi Sleng Teng* heralded the arrival of the digital sound in dancehall.

The adversarial or sound-clash element of the outdoor sound system included versioning – where different lyrics were spoken or sung over the same rhythm tracks and invoked call and response between the performers and the audience. In a 'sound clash', an antagonistic lyrical competition, the act of rhyming over a beat is a crucial aspect, with the emphasis on bringing something new or original to the battle. Performers will often throw down a lyrical challenge and 'send for' another artist. The clash was reworked and reconfigured for the enclosed dwellings of the UK. Over time, UK-based sound systems emerged and started to play other styles of music: swingbeat, R n B, soul and garage. It is possible to recognise the sonic remnants of dancehall DJs such as Cutty Ranks and Ninjaman in the early grime clashes.

Enterprise and resistance

In Jamaica, sound systems and the accompanying dances were a predominantly working-class activity. With a sonic emphasis on the bass and the treble, large speakers played the music at high volume. As well as entertainment, the sound systems provided a way for people within and outside the music setting to earn an income. They did not just play records: they produced their own artists and released music on their own labels. These opportunities were not only as artists, distributors and event promoters (with these roles often being interchangeable), but also from allied activities such as the sale of food, alcohol and souvenirs (Witter 2004).

Sound systems formed an integral part of both the blues dance and the legal rave; their presence attracted a paying audience to an event. In the UK, these proceedings were held indoors and because the bass was heavy, and often supplemented by whistles, foghorns and exhortations for the crowd to 'lick wood',[7] it was very loud. In 1970s Britain, Sunday was still a day of rest. This created conflict between the participants and event promoters and the regulating authorities. The public performance of black music such as grime and its predecessors has always been problematic in England. For instance, in the 1970s and early 1980s reggae music had little public presence and was rarely played on licensed radio. To listen to it, one had to go out into the public sphere, underground to a blues dance (an unregistered event, sometimes hosted in a domestic dwelling, where on payment of an entrance fee, it was possible to dance the night away) or a nightclub that specialised in that type of music. At that time, the 'sus' law[8] formed part of an overall project to contain and control black youth (Scarman *et al.* 1982). Although this law is no longer in use (it has been replaced by Section 1 of the 1984 Police and Criminal Evidence Act – PACE), current evidence suggests that young black men are still up to seven times more likely to be subjected to stop and search (Van Bueren and Woolley 2010). At that time, it was common for the police to raid venues on the pretext of illegal drug possession and consumption, and participants at reggae events became an easy and lazy shorthand for 'dangerous individuals smoking illegal substances' (Bradley 2000, p. 428).

In more recent times, in 2009 the Metropolitan Police introduced the Promotion Event Risk Assessment Form (or Form 696), ostensibly as a mechanism to reduce serious crime (Metropolitan Police SC9 Proactive Intelligence Unit 2009). Event promoters were asked to provide the name, date of birth and contact details of every artist performing at an event. They were also required to specify the genre of music that would be played. This led to a large number of cancellations for urban music events of any kind, but particularly grime (Hancox 2009; Hancox 2010; Izundu 2010). In Foucauldian terms, crime prevention procedures and processes were being used to pin down and partition those who wanted to perform at or attend urban music events (Foucault 1991).

Pirate radio stations playing this type of music were seen as a threat that needed to be eradicated or curtailed, because they were presumed to be sites of illegal drug use and their activities were presumed to interfere with the legitimate pursuits of the emergency services (Wroe 1993; BBC News Channel 2007; Sherwin 2007). The internecine acrimony within and between grime crews is well documented; for example Bashy, a north London artist, launched a vitriolic verbal attack on Ghetts, an east London artist, accusing him of 'talking loose on [the set of] Mr. Wong's video shoot'. Ghetts's response was to tell Bashy in no uncertain terms that he was at 'the bottom of the food chain' (streetzinctv 2008). Furthermore, Wiley was verbally challenged live on air at a pirate radio station by MC God's Gift and members of the Mucky Wolfpack crew (viceland 2006; KicksAndSnaresUK 2010), and there is the now infamous clash between Crazy Titch and Dizzee Rascal on a rooftop at Déjà Vu, another pirate radio station (chocdip 2006). This seemingly chaotic conduct left the authorities anxious to control and restrict performance of this genre.

The fact that grime could not be performed live is perhaps why, in *Pirates Dilemma*, Matt Mason called this genre a meme without a scene: it could not be played publicly, so had nowhere to go (Mason 2008). But unlike its predecessor, garage, grime did not vanish; instead, the performance locations for this creative expression spread outwards, and advances in technology allowed audiences to be established first in the London suburbs, then across the UK, and then to Europe, North America and Africa. With a distinct sound and new locations, participants' activities began to disseminate outwards, first across the UK and then across Europe. At the same time, Rinse FM, the pirate radio station that had pioneered garage and then grime since its first broadcast, became legal (rinsefm 2012a; rinsefm 2012b). Logan Sama's long-running show on Kiss FM made it possible for grime and other emerging urban music genres to be accessed by a wider audience. Rinse FM also provided a route to regular paid work in the formal economy for some former pirate DJs, including Marcus Nasty and Sir Spyro.

Independent artists in the grime music scene have used the Internet to disseminate their creative output at a local, national and global level. Technological advances have meant that the traditional recorded music industry has evolved from a local and personal activity shared with co-present others to one in which an artist can now build a direct and immediate relationship with an audience

(Baym 2010). Record companies no longer have a tight control over the distribution of digital material. Urban music artists can promote online personas that can be exchanged in a reciprocal or circular way. The Internet has empowered artists, enabling them to transcend distance and reach large audiences without the intervention of the big three record labels. A space has been created in which UK urban music artists can match the creative and economic success of the Jamaican recorded music industry. Jamaica punches way above its weight in terms of the outward global impact of its recorded music industry: by the late 1990s, annual sales of reggae music represented 4 per cent of Jamaican GDP (McMillan 2005, p. 2). Innovation in this sector came through the 'creative city' or 'creative cluster' of Kingston, which housed an estimated 2,000 artists in one small area. Record producers were therefore able to draw on a wide pool of talent. Whereas the 'Big Four'[9] (now big three) record companies produced, manufactured and distributed recordings and licensed music rights, Jamaica had a large number of small, specialised organisations involved in the different aspects of making and distributing a recording. In addition, the recording studios were clustered in a specific area and musicians moved freely among different companies (McMillan 2005, p. 15). This movement enabled the flow of musical ideas and innovation. The Internet has enabled the Kingston model to occur locally and be disseminated on a much wider scale, without the need for intermediaries. It is entirely possible for independent recording artists in the urban music economy, such as JME and Griminal, to establish an audience and a fan base through having an online presence (ManBetterKnow 2011; 360records09 2009). Creative clusters, in this context, are street corners, or housing estates in 'the ends', or local neighbourhoods rather than the creative hubs of Shoreditch or the Silicon Roundabout (Kingsley 2011). In these clusters, independent recording artists share ideas and resources and collaborate to create and disseminate artistic products/music.

Working together: collaboration and conviviality in the grime music scene

Many grime artists work cooperatively across postcodes, genres and crews, which runs counter to the stereotypical image of an urban music aesthetic segregated by area and affiliation. Jammer, formerly of N.A.S.T.Y crew, is a veteran of the grime scene. He works as an independent but also collaborates frequently with Boy Better Know (BBK). With his Lord of the Mics (LOTM) series, Jammer has recorded many of grime's luminaries clashing in his iconic basement setting. Partnership and collaboration is a key organising principle for this sector. It has enabled simultaneous operation within the formal and informal economic sectors. For example, some members of Roll Deep are now embedded firmly in the mainstream music industry: DJ Target presents a radio programme on BBC 1XTRA (BBC 1Xtra 2013), while N.A.S.T.Y crew have an internet radio station with DJs broadcasting from a wide geographical area, including Malaysia, Italy, Toronto, Rotterdam, Montreal, San Francisco and the Czech Republic, as well as across the UK.

Boy Better Know (BBK) is a north London crew who often work in partnership with artists from Roll Deep. Furthermore, artists in and out of these crews work together, often for no payment,to circulate their creative product to a wider audience. This collaborative practice is clearly illustrated by a Boy Better Know track, *Duppy*, released in 2006. Produced by Skepta, it illuminates the collective work in this sector, in that it features vocals by Skepta and JME from BBK; Wiley from Roll Deep; Jammer (formerly of N.A.S.T.Y. crew); Footsie from Newham Generals; Bossman out of Meridian Crew; Bearman, a south London MC; former Roll Deep member, Trim; and a veteran garage music artist by the name of MC Creed. This combined effort runs counter to suggestions that UK urban music is a highly individualised endeavour conducted in bounded territories or postcode silos. In more recent times, Tinchy Stryder, an east London MC of Ghanaian origin, produced a track in 2010 called *Game Over* (tinchystrydertv 2010a). It includes six other artists – Giggs, Professor Green, Tinie Tempah, Devlin, Example and Chipmunk – from a range of cultural backgrounds, including Jamaican, white English and Nigerian. Each performer takes their spot in front of the camera and delivers their lines in the allotted time, putting their individual style and lyrics over the beat. The remix for this track was released shortly afterwards and it featured both signed and independent artists (tinchystrydertv 2010b).[10]

Grime draws on, and is informed by, the cultural intermixture that takes places between black and white working-class youth on street corners and housing estates. As a cultural practice, it therefore raises a question with regards to who is accountable for what is said about these localities. In the same year that *Game Over* was released, Professor Green, a white MC from Clapton in the London borough of Hackney, released a video for his award-winning track *Jungle* (NME 2011) featuring the vocals of a white Irish singer, Maverick Sabre (professorgreentv 2010). Verse one begins with Professor Green announcing: 'Welcome to Hackney'. Then looping images show hooded and sometimes masked black men perpetrating acts of criminality and violence. Two white artists are detached observers throughout the video, showing an unwitting and probably terrified public what 'real life' is like in this jungle called Hackney. It is not clear whether Professor Green had artistic control of the visual rendering of the track, but the lyrics likening certain members of the Hackney population to hungry apes are firmly credited to him.

Professor Green uses black street vernacular to speak from the position of a cultural insider and urges 15 million YouTube viewers to look, but keep moving, because 'it's wild out here'. This track was subject to commentary from black artists, including Rapper Akala, who highlighted and articulated the racial mechanics of this gaze and located *Jungle* in its economic and political context (IAmBirmingham 2012). Akala asserts that the UK music industry cannot be free from racism even if, as Professor Green later insists, it is a misreading of both the song and the video; he is simply presenting his truth from the perspective of his upbringing on an estate in that location (Galea 2012). The debate illustrates how black artists in this sector are still subject to the ethnically coded stereotypes that accompany inhabitants of a stigmatised community and the territorial fixation that views the spaces they occupy as undesirable badlands (Wacquant 2007, p. 236).

Participants in the urban music economy were early adopters of emerging technology, particularly social media. Grime came of age in the YouTube era (and the time of the camera phone). It therefore became easier and more accessible for people to film and broadcast their own videos. Advances in technology have made it possible for connectivity between pirate radio stations, club events and social media as a way to market and promote urban music of all kinds, including grime. Participation in this arena therefore requires learning and updating technological skill, working in collaboration and understanding how to exchange or barter goods and services. Combined with accessible broadcasting, first through Channel U and subsequently Channel AKA, a unique opportunity has been created to record a story and share it with the world. The street has found its own uses for this technology, and my informants have used it as a way to reinvent themselves.

Growing up under the influence: charting a musical heritage

In the media, black lives are scrutinised and harshly judged. A notion of absence pervades the discourse on families of Caribbean heritage, an absence that some policymakers would argue translates into a dearth of positive male role models, which in turn has a detrimental effect on the life chances of black boys and young black men in particular. The Reach Project and its follow-up report cited the lack of role models and mentors as a crucial determinant factor for low levels of aspiration and achievement (Communities and Local Government 2007; Communities and Local Government 2011). Instead, they suggest that we need to move away from profiling achievements from music and sport and consider success in a wider context. In other words,

> Success by 2020 would mean ... Black men are represented in a significant number of powerful positions, ... high-ranking judicial positions, ... companies in the FTSE 250 ... prevalent media stereotypes of ... sporting or music stars, or gang members, should fade as Black men become more visible'
>
> (Communities and Local Government 2011, p. 4)

The Joseph Rowntree report into low educational achievement found that that black boys are more likely to have lower levels of attainment at GCSE than any other ethnic group and are also more likely be excluded from school. Finally, it concludes that black men are less likely to attend university at age 19 and are over-represented in prisons and young offender institutions (Cassen and Kingdon 2007, p. 4). It concludes that 'it is apparent that something has been arresting the progress of Caribbean students – boys in particular – [because] even if they start out well, they may come to grief later' (Cassen and

Kingdon 2007, p. 9). Other researchers argue that black pupils always perform worse than white ones, and suggest that even when class is accounted for '25% of black boys got five good GCSEs compared to 43.5% of white boys' (Sergeant 2009; BBC Online 2010).

These reports negate the positive influence handed down and passed on by familial connections in the urban music sector. When I interviewed him in 2009, Ian, the DJ whose words open the chapter, told me that his father was a UK reggae singer and had had some commercial success in the 1980s. Another informant, Oliver, a pioneer in the UK garage and grime scene now operating as an independent recording artist, explained that his father was a reggae and sound system DJ who had started out on pirate radio and who also had had a long stint on a national radio station. At different times over a two-year period, I interviewed four brothers, Victor, James, Edward and Andrew, who were all heavily involved in the urban music economy (as MCs and DJs playing a variety of genres, including grime). Each of them informed me that their father was a musician, a drummer in a reggae band of many years standing. Edward said 'I grew up around music, you could say that music is my backbone'. David, an independent recording artist who was also a member of a north London crew, described being part of a fabric of music, sounds and performance. He told me: 'I'm not sure when I started, my brother was a DJ, my Dad was a DJ, music took hold of me'.

Brian, a 40-year-old radio and club DJ, explained to me how being part of his father's sound system from a young age gave him a positive foundation:

> My Dad is a sound man, so he's got his own sound system, so I've been in it since I was a kid, really. I mean, we used to get up to stuff, but what saved me was actually the music really, when I was a teenager. Because my Dad had the sound, that was the weekend treat, and he used to play up and down the country, and rather than getting caught up with the police and getting into stuff I shouldn't be getting into, I was going up to Birmingham, to Manchester, to Liverpool. Get ready, jump in the back of the truck and that was it.

I met Peter when he was performing at a club night in Ayia Napa, Cyprus. A 34-year-old member of a UK sound system and a DJ on national radio, Peter told me that 'My Dad was a musician and had a recording studio, my Mum was a singer as well, my brother was a music collector, my uncles were DJs, I literally grew up around music'. Kevin had been a DJ and was now operating as an MC. He spoke effusively about his apprenticeship, starting out as a DJ at the age of 13 and ultimately getting a weekly residency with his crew members in a nightclub in Clapton, because the owner – an older black man of Caribbean heritage – saw their potential:

> We played there every Friday. The owner, he took a liking to us and he said 'yeah, I'll make you resident every Friday', so that's where we got, that's

how we learned basically how to deal with different audiences, cos we were playing to people who were much older than us. So they didn't really want to hear the jungle; they really wanted to hear some good reggae, some good soul, and they want you to play it right. They don't want you to be chatting things over the top of it. That's where we learnt our discipline, 'cos we were so young, by the time we got into garage, we were like seasoned DJs.

The informants in this book have used grime music to articulate their living conditions, to speak of the lack of opportunity and to create a route to employment through enterprise. Through serving apprenticeships with sound systems and grime crews, honing their craft by watching and working with others, these practitioners have used their creativity to establish ways to learn and earn. Bourdieu suggests that people attempt what is possible, and what is possible is based on what is seen around you. Engaging in this economy allows creative practitioners to see and experience the world in a more substantial way; therefore the possiblities for improvement and exit increase (Jenkins 2002). What Nigel Thrift calls 'the crushing weight of economic circumstance' in the 'cramped worlds in which many people are forced to live their lives' (Thrift 2007, p. 20) has been disrupted by participation in the urban music economy.

Conclusion

The opening decade of the twenty-first century saw grime music emerge from the street corners and council estates of urban east London, where the offspring of Commonwealth migrants and the young white working class socialised and congregated, drawing on Jamaican sound system culture and practice and dance-hall rhythms to create a uniquely English sound. Against a continuing backdrop of economic constraint – the 2008 global financial crisis, subsequent austerity policies and rising unemployment – young black men continued to serve apprenticeships in grime crews. In so doing, they honed their craft, writing lyrics, making beats and sharing resources, and creating a complex intermixture of innovative ideas and practice. Taking a pragmatic approach to the acquisition of technological skills, grime artists became experts in the use of social media and online and digital TV channels. Although control and curtailment of live performance made it seem that grime would disappear, it flourishes and remains a site where artists can work together, or independently, often sharing resources, ideas and information, firing off sparks of genius (and mediocrity) via 'clashes', 'sends', downloads and videos that a much wider world now has a taste for. Gaining direct feedback from fans and peers means that grime music is an enduring presence in the UK urban music economy. Grime, however, has a global reach that should not be underestimated.

Of course, there is a racial and ethnic dimension to all of this: grime output is still generally perceived as an incitement to violence (particularly when it is the product of young black men). The myth of missing role models in black families and black communities is a well-worn trope. Over a five-year period, I spoke to young men who had been immersed in music, who looked around at what their cousins/uncles/fathers/brothers were doing and found something positive to emulate. I make no great claims to exploding these myths; however, this is an underwritten story that needs to be told. Grime music has a social, economic and symbolic value and it allows for mobility as well as the creation of new identities. It does not flow in line within national borders. Instead, it moves back and forth, crossing boundaries but retaining the same distinctive sound. An exploration of grime exposes the web of relationships and business activities in the informal urban music economy. Its origins, practice and dissemination lie within the black Atlantic construct.

Notes

1 Chuck D – from rap group Public Enemy is credited with this analysis about the significance of rap music for those living in US forgotten black communities. The comment appears in various formations.
2 Paul Gilroy's black Atlantic concept is a heuristic device that challenges existing notions of nationality, authenticity and cultural integrity and allows for an analysis of the hybrid forms of creative expression produced predominantly by those from the black diaspora. These hybrid cultural forms draw on the Caribbean, North America and Africa and have been reworked for and in Britain. Through this concept, it is possible to explore the terrain between the camps of 'black' and 'white'. Within this context, cultural expression does not flow in line within national borders; instead it moves back and forth crossing boundaries and changing shape. It provides a way to analyse transnational and intercultural flow of creative expression. This analysis has a global significance as it can be used to explore the remaking of ethnic identities. For black Britons, an intermixture of distinct cultural forms has enabled the creation of a compound culture from disparate sources. New black vernacular creative expression and hybridised identities have been created from this intermixture.
3 The artistic differences are contested but seem to centre on the timing of an album release.
4 From chart success in 2009, Tinchy Stryder, aka Kwasi Danquah, is a frequent visitor to reality TV including ITV's I'm a Celebrity and All Star Mr & Mrs in 2015.
5 On 24 March 2009, Channel U had a change of ownership and now broadcasts as Channel AKA.
6 Some well-known examples of sound systems from the 1970s to the early 1990s are: 4 Play, 5th Avenue, 90%, Abashanti, Active Force, After Dark, AK, BIPA, Boogie Bunch, Caveman Boogie, CFFM, Channel One, Chicken, Confunkion, Count Shelly, Count Suckle, Drop Squad, Duke Neville, Duke Vin, Fatman, Firin' Squad, Frontline, Fun Bunch, Gal Flex, Gaz's Rocking Blues, Gemi Magic, Hyper ESQ, Ill Kids, Jah Observer, Jah Tubby's, Jamdown Rocker, Java, Jungle Man, King Alfa, King Tubby's, Latin Rave, Lord Koo's, Lord Sam, Love Injection, Mafiatone, Mellow Prime Time, Metro Glory, Midnight Express, Mistri, the Mistri Crew, One Love, Pioneer, Players, Pleasure Roadshow, Quaker City, Rampage, Rough but Sweet, Sancho Panza, Saxon, Secret Rendezvous, Shaka, Sir Christopher Kebra Negus, Sir Coxsone, Sir Higgins, Soul II Soul, Sovereign, Special FX, Special Touch, Studio 1, Studio Express 365, Sufferer, the Thunderstorm, Tonka, Touch of Class, Trenchtown, Unity, Urban Rockers, Virgo, Wasifia.
7 Beating the walls and doors with your hands as a sign of appreciation.
8 The 'sus' laws, as they were commonly known, were actually Section 4 of the Vagrancy Act 1824, which the police used to stop and search those they suspected of

committing a crime. It was held to be a key factor in the Brixton and other inner-city riots in 1981.
9 The 'Big Four' record companies held a 75 per cent global market share of the recorded music industry: Universal, 24 per cent; Sony BMG, 25 per cent; EMI, 13 per cent; and Warner, 13 per cent.
10 The Game Over Remix featured Ghetts, Slix, Griminal, Dot Rotten, Fuda Guy, Wretch 32, Roachee, Maxsta and Tinchy Stryder.

References

360records09, 2009. *Griminal – Invincible (OFFICIAL VIDEO – HD)*, Available at: www.youtube.com/watch?v=5gpBIfqvojA&feature=youtube_gdata_player [accessed 20 December 2010].

Baym, N.K., 2010. *Personal connections in the digital age*, Cambridge, UK and Malden, MA: Polity.

BBC 1Xtra, 2013. BBC Radio 1Xtra – DJ Target. Available at: www.bbc.co.uk/programmes/b0071ryj [accessed 22 December 2013].

BBC News Channel, 2003a. Minister attacks rap lyrics. *BBC*. Available at: http://news.bbc.co.uk/1/hi/wales/2752681.stm [accessed 14 April 2012].

BBC News Channel, 2003b. Rapper Rascal wins Mercury Prize. *BBC*. Available at: http://news.bbc.co.uk/1/hi/entertainment/music/3092520.stm [accessed 11 September 2010].

BBC News Channel, 2007. Pirate radio 'risk to aircraft'. *BBC*. Available at: http://news.bbc.co.uk/1/hi/england/london/6617765.stm [accessed 24 August 2011].

BBC Online, 2010. Half of young black people unemployed. Available at: http://news.bbc.co.uk/1/hi/uk/8468308.stm.

Beauman, N., 2006. Is violence holding grime back?, *Guardian*. Available at: www.theguardian.com/music/musicblog/2006/nov/06/isviolenceholdinggrimeback [accessed 20 October 2013].

Benton, G. and Gomez, E.T., 2011. *Chinese in Britain, 1800-present*, Houndmills: Palgrave Macmillan.

Bradley, L., 2000. *Bass culture: When reggae was king*, London, UK: Viking.

British Grime/Garage Music History, 2013. *2001 Rolldeep B2B Nasty Crew 92.3 Deja Vu FM*, Available at: www.youtube.com/watch?v=7JVCGsbtm94&feature=youtube_gdata_player [accessed 4 May 2015].

Cassen, R. and Kingdon, G., 2007. *Tackling low educational achievement*, York: Joseph Rowntree Foundation.

chocdip, 2006. *Dizzee Rascal and Crazy Titch hypin to eachother*, Available at: www.youtube.com/watch?v=hyLkLHY2LuQ&feature=youtube_gdata_player [accessed 20 December 2010].

Communities and Local Government, 2007. REACH Report. Available at: www.communities.gov.uk/publications/communities/reachreport [accessed 15 September 2010].

Communities and Local Government, 2011. Reach Update Report: Progress against the five recommendations of the REACH report into raising the aspirations and attainment of Black boys and young Black men.

D, C. and Jah, Y., 1997. *Fight the power: Rap, race and reality with Yusuf Jah*, Edinburgh: Payback Press.

First Sight, 2002. Race adviser attacks So Solid Crew. Available at: http://news.bbc.co.uk/1/hi/entertainment/music/1846237.stm [accessed 14 April 2012].

Foucault, M., 1991. *Discipline and punish: The birth of the prison*, London, UK: Penguin.

Galea, K., 2012. Akala and Professor Green involve maverick sabre in heated twitter debate. *MTV UK*. Available at: www.mtv.co.uk/music/urban/6369-akala-and-professor-green-involve-maverick-sabre-in-heated-twitter-debate [accessed 22 December 2013].

Gilroy, P., 1996. *The Black Atlantic*, London: Verso.

Hampson, S., 2009. Interview: Geeneus – FACT magazine: Music and art. Available at: www.factmag.com/2009/01/01/interview-geeneus [accessed 11 September 2010].

Hancox, D., 2009. Public enemy no 696. *Guardian*. Available at: www.guardian.co.uk/culture/2009/jan/21/police-form-696-garage-music [accessed 16 June 2013].

Hancox, D., 2010. Grime: Banished from physical London. Available at: http://dan-hancox.blogspot.co.uk/2010/02/grime-banished-from-physical-london.html [accessed 16 June 2013].

Hancox, D., Lea, T. and Mr Beatnick, 2013. Stand up tall: A round table debate about Dizzee Rascal's Boy in Da Corner and the birth of grime – FACT Magazine: Music News, New Music. Available at: www.factmag.com/2013/08/22/stand-up-tall-a-round-table-debate-about-dizzee-rascals-boy-in-da-corner-and-the-birth-of-grime/ [accessed 6 October 2013].

Hill Collins, P., 2006. New commodities, new consumers: Selling blackness in a global marketplace. *Ethnicities*, 6(3), pp. 297–317.

IAmBirmingham, 2012. *Akala on Professor Green and racism*. Available at: www.youtube.com/watch?v=KItxO8AffE0&feature=youtube_gdata_player [accessed 21 December 2013].

i-D Staff, 2015. Danny weed and dj target discuss the history of grime. *i-D*. Available at: https://i-d.vice.com/en_gb/article/danny-weed-and-dj-target-discuss-the-history-of-grime [accessed 8 July 2015].

Izundu, C.C., 2010. Police defend club check forms. *BBC*. Available at: www.bbc.co.uk/newsbeat/10174673 [accessed 16 June 2013].

Jackson, J., 2005. Ready to blow. *Guardian*. Available at: www.guardian.co.uk/music/2005/apr/24/popandrock3 [accessed 14 April 2012].

Jenkins, R., 2002. *Pierre Bourdieu*, 2nd edn, Routledge.

Jones, S., 2010. The grime report: Rap music feud behind gun violence in Birmingham. Available at: http://thegrimereport.blogspot.co.uk/2010/06/rap-music-feud-behind-gun-violence-in.html [accessed 20 October 2013].

KicksAndSnaresUK, 2010. *Wiley 'getting rushed' on Rinse FM back in the day*, Available at: www.youtube.com/watch?v=w5Ahi5x5xe4&feature=youtube_gdata_player [accessed 7 July 2012].

Kingsley, P., 2011. Tech City: The magic roundabout. *Guardian*. Available at: www.theguardian.com/business/2011/nov/27/tech-city-digital-startups-shoreditch [accessed 16 March 2014].

London Borough of Hackney, 2005. Hackney local improvement plan.

London Borough of Newham, 2005. Newham local implementation plan.

London Borough of Tower Hamlets, 2005. Tower Hamlets local implementation plan.

ManBetterKnow, 2011. *Jme – 'JME'*. Available at: www.youtube.com/watch?v=71edyENuW6U&feature=youtube_gdata_player [accessed 22 June 2013].

Mason, M., 2008. *The pirate's dilemma: How hackers, punk capitalists, graffiti millionaires and other youth movements are remixing our culture and changing our world*, London, UK: Penguin.

McMillan, J., 2005. Trench Town rock: The creation of Jamaica's music industry. Unpublished conference paper, 13 February 2004. Stanford, CA: Stanford Graduate School of Business, Case IB.

Metropolitan Police SC9 Proactive Intelligence Unit, 2009. Promotion event risk assessment form 696.

Muggs, J., 2010. Violent grime on the increase. Available at: www.theartsdesk.com/new-music/violent-grime-increase [accessed 20 October 2013].

Neighbourhood Statistics, 2007. Trend view. Available at: www.neighbourhood.statistics. gov.uk/dissemination/LeadTrendView [accessed 30 January 2011].

NME, 2011. Professor Green's 'Jungle' voted Shockwaves NME Awards Best Dance-floor Filler. *NME.COM*. Available at: www.nme.com/news/professor-green/55129 [accessed 22 December 2013].

Plunkett, J., 2003. Blunkett to target rap producers. *Guardian*. Available at: www. guardian.co.uk/media/2003/jan/06/radio.politics [Accessed 14 April 2012].

professorgreentv, 2010. *Professor Green ft. Maverick Sabre – Jungle (HD) [Official Video]*. Available at: www.youtube.com/watch?v=GLfEU5lelUM&feature=youtube_gdata_player [accessed 21 December 2013].

rinsefm, 2012a. *18 Years of Rinse | 1994 : Geeneus*. Available at: www.youtube.com/watch?v=qYeWYtzCpoI&feature=youtube_gdata_player [accessed 28 September 2012].

rinsefm, 2012b. *18 Years of Rinse | 2009: Marcus Nasty*. Available at: www.youtube. com/watch?v=xI8aA9ab_yg&feature=youtube_gdata_player [accessed 28 September 2012].

Rose, T., 1994. *Black noise: Rap music and black culture in contemporary America*, Hanover, NH: Wesleyan University Press.

Scarman, L.S., Great Britain and Home Office, 1982. *The Brixton disorders, 10–12 April 1981: The Scarman report: Report of an inquiry*, Harmondsworth, Middlesex and New York: Penguin Books.

Sergeant, H., 2009. *Wasted: The betrayal of white working-class and black Caribbean boys*, London, UK: Centre for Policy Studies.

Sherwin, A., 2007. Pirate radio DJs risk prosecution to fight gun and knife crime. *Times Online*. Available at: www.timesonline.co.uk/tol/news/uk/article2288801.ece [accessed 24 August 2011].

So Solid Crew, 2006. Welcome to www.sosolid.co.uk. Available at: www.sosolid.co.uk/ lisaharveyromeo.html [accessed 13 April 2012].

streetzinctv, 2008. *Grime Beef (Pt1) – Bashy, Ghetto, Wiley, Marcus Nasty, Crazy Titch, Dizzie Rascal (Streetzinctv)*. Available at: www.youtube.com/watch?v=ZvT6GJXMn6 o&feature=youtube_gdata_player [accessed 29 January 2011].

Tames, R., 2006. *London: A cultural history*, New York: Oxford University Press.

Thrift, N., 2007. *Non-representational theory: Space, politics, affect*, Abingdon, UK and New York: Routledge.

tinchystrydertv, 2010a. *Tinchy Stryder: Game over feat. Giggs, Professor Green, Tinie Tempah, Devlin, Example and Chipmunk*. Available at: www.youtube.com/watch?v= 3wpCf0FsZKQ&feature=youtube_gdata_player [accessed 20 December 2010].

tinchystrydertv, 2010b. *Tinchy Stryder – Game Over Remix – Official Video*, Available at: www.youtube.com/watch?v=x3jMmIZDQv0&feature=youtube_gdata_player [accessed 20 December 2010].

Van Bueren, G. and Woolley, S., 2010. *Stop and think: A critical review of the use of stop and search powers in England and Wales*, London, UK: Equality and Human Rights Commission.

viceland, 2006. Grimewatch: Wiley vs. God's Gift. *VICE*. Available at: www.vice.com/en_uk/read/grimewatch-wiley-vs-gods-gift-5 [accessed 5 February 2014].

Wacquant, L., 2007. *Urban outcasts: A comparative sociology of advanced marginality*, Cambridge, UK: Polity.

Witter, M., 2004. *Music and the Jamaican economy*, Prepared for UNCTAD/WIPO.

Wroe, M., 1993. Pirate radio stations 'linked to drugs': Illegal broadcasters used as front for crime, regulator says *Independent*. Available at: www.independent.co.uk/news/uk/pirate-radio-stations-linked-to-drugs-illegal-broadcasters-used-as-front-for-crime-regulator-says-1461770.html [accessed 24 August 2011].

Part II

Creative enterprise as social practice

3 Artist-entrepreneurs

Working for love and money

A lot of the people I grew up with are crackheads, drug dealers or dead. And these were the kids that were doing well. Everyone thought that would be me … music definitely changed my life, it gave me something to do.

(Victor, 33 – DJ – interviewed in 2010)

Introduction

A few miles from London's major financial districts, the inner East London boroughs of Tower Hamlets, Newham and Hackney still contain pockets of deep poverty. This is despite years of regeneration and redevelopment, including the development of creative hubs such as Tech City, which runs from the boundary of the City of London at Old Street to Queen Elizabeth Olympic Park. Nevertheless, for most young people in these boroughs access to good quality jobs and training is scarce. In a world where accreditation is of paramount importance for entry into work and further education, young people find themselves in a 'low pay, no pay' cycle (Shildrick *et al.* 2010), inhabiting low-income jobs that do not offer a living wage or coming under the auspices of an increasingly punitive welfare benefits system.

Work is a rite of passage into adulthood; however, structural economic changes since the 1980s have contributed to increased levels of youth unemployment. This is compounded by an education system that is continually being adjusted, 'improved' and remade. Within this system, those who fail to achieve the required levels of qualification often become classified as NEET. The activities of those who inhabit this category of deficit are rendered invisible by a discourse that is racialised and classed. What these young people are doing, in terms of work, education and training is rarely recorded; this is therefore my main focus in this chapter. I also introduce the concept of the artist-entrepreneur to describe someone who resides in 'the ends', or poor neighbourhoods, with very few resources, and who creates work for themselves or others, or both. Through observation and interview, I foreground the working lives of artist-entrepreneurs in the urban music economy as they utilise their creative practice to make a place for themselves.

The East End of London: a moving picture

Over the last decade, the inner east London boroughs have undergone a shift: from being a post-industrial area scoring low on most economic and social indicators, they became the location for the majority of the London 2012 Olympics (BBC London 2008). Despite the significant redevelopment accompanying this mammoth project,[1] three of the most deprived boroughs in London continue to be Hackney, Tower Hamlets and Newham. The Office for National Statistics (ONS) cites the east London Boroughs of Newham and Tower Hamlets as two of the most economically and socially deprived boroughs in the United Kingdom (London Borough of Tower Hamlets 2005; London Borough of Hackney 2005; London Borough of Newham 2005; MacRury and Poynter 2009). Although a recent report suggests that the unemployment rate has fallen, the number of those who are 'working poor' and rely on the state to maintain a living wage has grown (Aldridge *et al.* 2015).

Urban poverty in the UK has been a matter of public concern for generations (Hills 2010; Elkes 2013; Randhawa 2013). Social mobility in the UK is at its lowest level for decades; therefore opportunities for a way out of these environments are limited (Blanden and Machin 2007). The City of London, one of the major financial districts in the world, looms large in the midst of some of the poorest wards in the United Kingdom, offering a tantalising view of how the other half lives. Despite redevelopment and regeneration such as Canary Wharf, young people from Newham, Tower Hamlets and Hackney remain relatively socially and economically immobile (MacRury and Poynter 2009).

Work, education and training

Wage labour is a rite of passage from adolescence to adulthood and if one exists on the margins of the paid labour market it is possible that one will remain in a state of quasi-adolescence in which agency is curtailed and decisions are made on your behalf. In areas of high unemployment, all but the most basic occupations require a level of qualification for entry and progression. The low incomes afforded by these jobs do not, on the whole, provide a living wage, and are therefore subsidised by the government in the form of welfare benefits.

Parallels can be drawn with Patricia Hill Collins's analysis of the relationship between black American youth and hip-hop and UK black participants in the urban music sector. She argues that 'African-American youth [...] no longer needed for cheap unskilled labour in fields and factories, poor and working class black youth find few opportuntities in the large urban areas where most now reside' (Hill Collins 2006, p. 297). In the UK, the parents and grandparents of many of my respondents had come from the Caribbean and Africa to fill gaps in the labour market. Those subsequently born here had fewer gaps to fill, and in poor areas such as the east end of London there was less opportunity for semi-skilled and unskilled work. The structural economic changes of the 1980s had a negative impact on youth employment levels (Furlong and Cartmel 2007;

Murray and Gayle 2012). As Loic Wacquant argues, poor young people in general 'occupy unstable positions on the margins of the wage labour sphere' (2007, p. 51), and for young black men a 50 per cent unemployment rate is disproportionate and damaging (Ball *et al.* 2012).

The standard way for young people to achieve recognition is by undergoing programmes of learning leading to educational attainment and then to paid work in the formal economy. Education, training and the acquisition of skills have long been viewed as a fundamental pillar of economic reconstruction and growth. Indeed, in the UK they are deemed to be key components of the welfare state (Mac an Ghaill 1996; Willemse and de Beer 2012). Since the 1980s, there has been a climate of accredited educational achievement in the UK, and success for young people is measured by the acquisition of qualifications. Specifically, the attainment of five grade A*–C GCSEs provides a gateway to further and ultimately higher education opportunities.

Some authors also argue that higher educational achievement generally leads to better outcomes in later life, including higher earnings and a lower probability of falling foul of the criminal justice system (see Taylor 2005; Allen and Ainley 2007; Skidmore 2008; Shepherd 2010; Clifton and Cook 2012). Driven by an assumption that increased levels of education is the key to a successful economy, the Conservative-led coalition government continued with what Sally Tomlinson called the 'epidemic of policy making' that she says has dogged the education sector for the last four decades (2005, p. 90). The *Leitch Review of Skills* contended that Britain's continuing prosperity depended on ideas and fresh talent, particularly because globalisation and technological change mean that economic success in the twenty-first century demands 'higher levels of innovation, faster response to change and increased creativity' (Leitch 2006, p. 6). Educational attainment and skills development remain at the forefront of Conservative government policy.

The contradictions of 'the ends'

'The ends' is a colloquial term used by young people in urban settings to denote local, familiar neighbourhoods. Despite the focus on what is missing in 'the ends' in terms of material goods and a perceived lack of socio-economic aspiration, it can also be argued that these areas actually provide comfort zones and enable residents to acquire social capital. They provide validation, recognition, stability and safety, as well as the more commonly posited repressive geographies (Reynolds 2013). Locality matters. It contributes to one's sense of self and informs the way that people present themselves to others. In this context, locality is an actively created, mediated space in which young people, supported by technology, use the cultural construction of 'the ends' to create personas that have purpose, power and meaning. In the East End of London and in other inner-city areas, swagger, gesture and pose protect against possible local difficulties and indicate belonging. In poor communities with little or reduced economic capital, life is organised around the practical aspects of getting by. A theme of making money and being able to provide for oneself and others pervades this habitus. The drive to be seen to be a success leads to the pursuit of recognition, reputation and monetary reward. Victor, the 33-year-old DJ whose quote opens this chapter, had grown up in east London in the 1980s and 1990s. He described his 'ends' thus: 'If I'd allowed, you know what, your ends does kind of dictate how you behave and how you are in life, but then it's up to you as you grow older to think 'I don't want to be a part of that'. It corrupts you from an early age' (Victor, DJ – 33).

It has been suggested that centuries of exposure to racial oppression leads black men to use 'the streets' or, indeed, 'the ends' as an alternative method of socialisation (Oliver 2006). This in turn leads to the construction of masculine identities that emphasise toughness, sexual conquest and street hustling (Gilroy 1996). Indeed, there are elements of truth in this; yet on YouTube generally, and on niche online channels such as SBTV in particular, this same stigmatised community use performance to construct masculine identities that showcase and highlight excellence, social commentary and humour.

This playfulness is illustrated by a YouTube video featuring a Stratford grime MC, Crazy Titch, 'merkin', or lyrically clashing with a minicab driver (chocdip 2006). The majority of the film takes place in a minicab somewhere in east London. Positioned in the front passenger seat, Crazy Titch is having a discussion with the minicab driver about why he is being overcharged for the fare. The performance is filmed on a mobile phone, with the minicab driver mostly out of shot. He performs the role of the angry young black man and insists that because the minicab driver has tried to overcharge him (four pounds fifty instead of the agreed three pounds fifty), he will only pay what he thinks the fare is now worth. He tells him: 'How about I give you nothing, how about I give you fifty pence?' In the film, it appears that the minicab driver attempts to extract additional funds because he has observed that this young man has a bundle of cash, 'just because you see a couple pinkies [fifty pound notes], you get excited' before dropping a fifty-pence piece in the side of the door and leaving the vehicle.

This film was uploaded on YouTube in 2006. It has been viewed approximately half a million times and is still being commented on today. It is worth noting that in 2007, Crazy Titch (Carl Dobson) started serving a minimum thirty-year prison sentence under the joint enterprise legislation. Joint enterprise refers to the use of a 300-year-old law to ensure the sharing of responsibility for a crime, not only among those that participated, but also including those that were present. It has a disproportionate impact on young black men.[2] It serves to illustrate the discourse about young black men being a community to be feared, controlled and contained. Yet there is something about the nature of these 'ends', or toughened environments, that nourishes and nurtures at the same time as it represses.

In these marginal communities, the condition of being 'on road' is constituted through the act of hanging out on a street corner or housing estate, and more than likely participating in some low-level illicit or illegal activity. It is often read to go hand in hand with being in 'the ends'. While some writers suggest that being 'on road' is a liminal space where there is sovereignty and agency as well as freedom from a hostile society (Gunter 2010), it has also been argued that it can be a collection of 'panicky, chaotic, adrenalin filled experiences' where young people exist in a heightened state of anxious awareness (Earle 2011, p. 134). Earle posits the notion of 'kinetic elite'. For them, the road is less hazardous, and they are afforded comfortable travel, mobile working, secure income and multiple domestic possibilities. This kinetic elite enjoy a 'comfort of certainty of arrival as well as departure'; their journeys are not obstructed or curtailed by representatives of the state. On the other hand, the 'kinetic underclass' has a motto 'live fast, die young/get rich or die trying' (Earle 2011, p. 135), which armours them against a world where they are under surveillance by the state and excluded from a formal economy that has no place for them.

Nevertheless, the majority of my informants did not specifically allude to being 'on road'. Instead, they talked about their areas as locations of comfort as well as difficulty. In this context, 'the ends' were places that gave the informants a grounding in real life as well as a motivation to move on. Andrew, an independent recording artist who had been categorised as at risk of becoming NEET, thought long and hard after being asked to describe the area that he grew up in:

> [east London area] Not the greatest area, a lot of negative things about that area but it's not about that really, I just want to, I don't want to be a product of my environment, if you know what I'm saying
> (Andrew, 18 – MC/Recording Artist – interviewed in 2010)

David, a recording artist, business owner and university graduate, responded to the same question as follows:

> I grew up in [an area in north London] – 'it's as real as it gets for street life, you know what I'm saying, you see things like ... that you might not want your children to see, like obvious negative things – growing up. It's not a wealthy area but there are so many more positive things that I took out of it [...] whole way of life, the way it makes you think and the way that when you do better in life, how you appreciate it and what you take from it as well because you know what cards you were dealt in the first place. I don't know man, it's like a double-edged sword, both sides to it. So I would never say it was bad, I would never say it was definitely good because maybe I might not want my children to be brought up the same way.
> (David, 26 – Recording Artist/Business Owner – interviewed in 2011)

Prior to this, he had been animated in his responses, but this question made him pause for a while. As he spoke, he lowered his voice and he carefully crafted his response. Both Andrew and David were making their mark in the urban music economy and they inhabited identities as artists and entrepreneurs. 'The ends' mattered because of the grounding they felt it gave them, but they also aspired for exit and for people to recognise that they were more than their environment. Tracey Reynolds uses the concepts of getting on, getting by, getting stuck and staying put to articulate the desire to validate their original locations but not wanting to be stuck in a landscape of limited possibilities. In particular, 'staying put to get on' is seen as a specific choice that young people from these areas make (Reynolds 2013).

It can be argued that it is possible to 'get on' by taking your creative practice outside of 'the ends', and music can offer a way to do this. However, once this movement has been made, there is the potential for transformation , not only of the environment that has been left, temporarily or permanently, but also of the individual who is in some way altered by this process. Participation in the urban music economy enables a transcendence of the boundaries of 'the ends'. It is also conceivable that if you do not get on, you have the comfort and security of the ends to fall back on. But this movement is not in one direction only; people get by, get on and return – it is a continuous movement. I interviewed Quentin, a 32-year-old MC/vocalist twice, once in Ayia Napa in 2009 and in the following year in Silvertown, east London. His movement is from pirate to licensed radio, and he has worked through a range of music genres over the last ten years: jungle, drum and bass, garage and funky. Quentin is still a club host and has a fairly regular stint on a licensed – formerly pirate – radio station. Having started out working mainly in the informal music economy, he is now in formal paid employment, and music has become an additional extra: 'I used to do this [MC/ vocalist] as my nine to five but now I'm a financial consultant and it's the other way round' (Quentin, 34 – vocalist interviewed in 2010).

Participating in the urban music economy enables these young people to break free of existing identifications, such as NEET, that appear to be an enduring condition of 'the ends'. Indeed, a significant proportion of young people from BAME communities (particularly those of Caribbean or Bangladeshi descent) become NEET (Leitch 2006). The drive to be visible, not just as under-achievers and NEETs lacking in qualifications, certification and aspiration, but also as entrepreneurs, business owners, artists and performers requires an ongoing effort. For outliers, visibility and recognition are crucial for a positive sense of self. There is a continuing debate regarding men in crisis, with boys' underachievement in education and over-representation in crime at the forefront of this discussion (Bainbridge and Browne 2010; Hills 2010; Cunningham 2012; Bingham 2013). This debate has a racial and ethnic dimension; for example, the REACH project concluded that black boys and young black men face 'serious challenges in every sector of society; they are less likely to do well at school, more likely to be unemployed and much more likely to become involved in the criminal justice system' (Communities and Local Government 2009, p. 6).

Artist-entrepreneurs in their own words

Entrepreneurs have a distinctive presence. What they do in general and who they are as individuals create images of an entrepreneurial identity (Anderson and Warren 2011). Throughout the project, I met with entrepreneurs in the urban music economy who had a tacit knowledge of their audience. Their innovative use of technology has enabled them to turn their output into a commodity with enduring social and economic significance. The majority of my research inform-ants were young black men of Caribbean and African descent; therefore their economic behaviour needs to be understood in its specific contexts and locali-ties. Practitioners in this sector, particularly those from impoverished back-grounds, want to earn a living; getting paid is a key motivation: 'I want to make … proper, proper, money' (James, 25 – DJ – interviewed in 2008); 'Cos, if I'm doing a big club then I'm going to want more money, cos I know the promoters are making dosh' (Ian, 22 – DJ – interviewed in 2008).

In times of constraint, it has been suggested that entrepreneurs draw on their traits, tastes, abilities, experience and networks to establish sustainable business (Pickernell *et al.* 2013, p. 360). However, for artist-entrepreneurs in the urban music economy, constraint is often the default position, and although they have access to resources in terms of skills and competencies, they are often without recourse to finance. What is clear, however, is that within this social context making money and getting paid is a primary focus. Although the enthusiasm that the artists have for what they do is equally important, what is difficult to trans-late to the page in a written form is the love and passion that the artists have for what they do. The drive to perform is compelling, whether as MCs, DJs or vocal-ists. The following story gives a flavour.

Zac was one of my business contacts. He was responsible for organising the annual two-day London Borough of Newham Show.[3] After the 2008 show, Zac came to my office for a meeting and seemed surprised to find Andrew there, quietly working on his MySpace site. This is what Zac told me:

> At the Saturday event, three teenagers came to the side of the stage and started tapping on the fence. When Zac asked them what they wanted, they said they wanted to perform. He explained that the playlist and running order had been set months ago and he couldn't take them. They kept plead-ing, he kept saying no and in the end they went away. Half an hour later, one young man came back on his own. He asked again, 'Just five minutes and then I'll get off, I promise'. Zac, seeing that he was desperate to perform, eventually agreed that he could fill a three-minute gap as an artist had not turned up. Andrew – in Zac's words – worked the stage and crowd, hyping up the atmosphere. As the crowd sang his lyrics back to him, it was apparent that his work was well known. It wasn't until much later on that he realised that it was Andrew, the shy young man who worked in our office and said very little.

Andrew was an 18-year-old MC by the time I interviewed him, he described how it felt to move from being an underachieving student, labelled by the school as pre-NEET, to being on stage: I don't know what, I can't describe it, I can't put it into words, seeing people jump and get excited from the music I've written and performing, I don't know … it keeps me going, it makes me want to do more. (Andrew, 18 – MC – interviewed in 2010).

What this quote does not do is give a sense of the way Andrew's face lit up, the smile that played on his lips when he tried to describe the feeling of performing to an audience. Brian, a 40-year-old van driver and DJ, had started out in this field as a teenage 'box boy'[4] for his father's sound system:

> and if you like making people feel good, that is a good, great buzz, out of the music. You know what I mean. You don't have to present to a 10 million people crowd, but if you've got the capability of making people enjoy themselves, even a minimum crowd, I mean, that's all good anyway ... Yeah, you can't beat it.
>
> (Brian, 40 – DJ – interviewed in 2009)

My final interview was with Steven, a postgraduate who described himself as being NEET by the age of 22. Steven's entry into the grime genre came via listening to an MC from Dagenham – Devlin (James Devlin) – while researching his dissertation. This interest had also propelled him towards various unpaid internships and, subsequently, to becoming managing director of an online TV channel and video production company. What the interview transcript does not provide, though, is an indication of his enthusiasm and interest when Steven describes being part of an organisation where he can invest his energy and ideas – being part of something which was – in his words – magical.

Out and about: the urban music economy in east London

I carried out my primary ethnographic research in areas where race and poverty intersect. These 'ends' are produced as an alien space, populated by those who are dangerous, violent and impoverished. However, as Loic Wacquant eloquently articulates, they actually consist of ordinary people, doing ordinary, everyday things to make a life and improve their lot. From an outside perspective, he argues, it might appear to be beyond the norm, in other words, 'peculiar, quixotic and even aberrant' (Wacquant 2007, p. 50), but there is in fact a rationality, a meaning, a motivation and a purpose for what people do and how they go about it. How else is it possible to survive the privations of the social and economic landscape other than look for a niche, find something that you are good at and, above all, establish a way to create work and make money?

Nightclubbing in Shoreditch

Victor invited me to a club in Shoreditch, in the London borough of Hackney, where he was DJ'ing on the same bill as David Rodigan – at that time a Kiss FM radio DJ. David Rodigan is a white man, in his early sixties and a veteran of the reggae scene. This is not a sound clash, where a number of DJs or MCs will use new music to battle and win over the crowd. This is a standard nightclub format with a number of DJs playing a set on the night, with the most well regarded situated at the top of the bill. Victor has asked me to come to this event not only because he wants me to see him at work, but also because he needs some photographs taken for promotional material. Just before midnight, I meet up with my friend near Great Eastern Street, walk down the road and join the queue outside. The crowd is mainly white and under 30, so we are a little conspicuous, but fortunately there are a few other older heads who have come to see David Rodigan perform. Once inside, I realise that I have been to this place before, when it had another name. Downstairs, there were the usual low ceilings with a long bar at the back of the room. My friend and I had agreed in advance that we would take it in turns to take photos. When we first arrive, the DJ is playing 80's dancehall, and there is a mellow, friendly atmosphere. On the stroke of midnight, David Rodigan begins his set. He plays his first track with the announcement that 'This is the first track I played when Kiss went legal' – *Pirates* (AndyManch 2011). The place erupts. We move closer to the DJ box to get a better view of what is happening on the dance floor from the DJ's perspective. The club fills up quickly, and soon the dance floor is replete with revellers. Victor and his two MCs (one of whom was a former grime MC) position themselves at the back of the DJ booth. They watch while Rodigan plays, and clearly enjoy what they see and feel. It is a strange juxtaposition, a time-served veteran being observed by old hands from the grime scene. Once Rodigan finishes his set, another DJ fills the gap, playing mainly dubstep, and warms the audience up for Victor. I wonder how the genres would work together – dancehall and funky house – but once Victor starts to play, my doubts disappear. Victor's two MCs work the crowd, taking it in turns to hype them up, invoking call and response, while he mixes and chops up the beats. The atmosphere remains electric, excited and lively; people dance until the night ends. I leave at roughly 2 a.m. with chants of 'oggi, oggi, oggi'[5] ringing in my ears.

A music video shoot in Hoxton

Victor is an old hand in the urban music scene. Others in the sector have advanced from the first steps and continue to work hard to build a level of self-sufficiency. Harvey, an early grime pioneer, was a member of a Walthamstow-based crew who achieved national chart success while he was an unemployed teenager in 2001. I meet him in November 2011 with his then current crew shooting his latest music video in Hoxton. He describes the place he grew up in as a rough council estate, but he says 'it inspired me, gave me a drive, seeing poverty made me want to get out'. For Harvey, music is his passion as well as his livelihood. As well as creating and releasing his own tracks, he is paid for individual live performance in clubs and universities. He still has a career as an independent, unsigned recording artist, but he has recently developed a street clothing brand, selling caps and T-shirts. Harvey is using his music activities to promote his brand, which he sells online and in major retail outlets such as JD Sports and Selfridges. At the time of the interview, Harvey has engaged a well-known stage and screen actress to promote his clothing line. Harvey is a consummate performer, perfectly at ease in front of the camera. Midway through our interview, someone comes in to tell us that cars are being ticketed and towed away outside. Harvey rushes out, deals with the situation, makes sure his car is moved and then returns, picking up the conversation exactly where he left off. Harvey was twenty-eight at the time of the interview and had spent a decade establishing a solid base for his creative practice and enterprise. Many of my younger informants, although they had less experience, were rooted in their identities as artists and had started to make their mark in the urban music economy.

Making their mark: a music video shoot in Beckton

In July 2010, I observe Andrew on the set of his music video shoot. This takes place approximately two miles from City Airport, on an industrial estate in Beckton. Andrew is filming his latest video for a digital TV channel. Edward, another of my informants, is due to feature in a 'hood' video[6] that is also planned to be filmed on the same set later that evening. I recognise one of the many young men who are on set – he was a former pupil at a primary school where I had been a school governor in the late 1990s. I locate Andrew's personal assistant (PA), who is coordinating the video shoot. Andrew is being styled for the first scene, and I manage to have a few words with him before he goes into performance mode.

While the PA, runners and director prepare for the shoot, the young men waiting to participate in the hood video relax with a few drinks and by performing some impromptu freestyling.[7] The model for the main video waits with them, and one of the young men approaches her. She is clearly much older than him, but he confidently assures her that he is twenty-two. The badinage goes back and forth until one of the other young men announces loudly, 'he's only 16'. This prompts raucous laughter from the crowd, and the young woman walks away shaking her head. For a while there is a certain amount of tension in the air, the banter becomes more heated and the would-be lothario starts to remove his jacket in preparation for a physical confrontation. The other young men step in and calm him down. Then there is a different laughter, and the mood lightens. As the evening wears on the freestyles become more strident, bawdy and explicit, and the language takes on a tougher turn. Finally, at about 1 a.m., fully energised and refreshed, this group goes outside to start filming their video. Meanwhile, at the other end of the warehouse, Andrew continues shooting take after take, unperturbed by the other activities on set. He is focused and professional and gets on with the job in hand. A runner is called to apply petroleum jelly to his lips to stop them drying out and to bring water to stop him dehydrating. As I observe him, I reflect on how far he has travelled from the quiet boy categorised as unmanageable by his school who had spent a year doing work experience in my office.

I note that the video director is a young white woman called Fiona, and later follow this up to see if she would be willing to be interviewed. I have a brief conversation with John, an independent recording artist who comes to provide a cameo for the main music video. John is a former member of an east London grime crew who had been signed and then dropped by a major record label. John grew up in Plaistow in the London borough of Newham. He tells me how his career as an MC has taken him out of 'the ends'. But, he explains, although he is tired – he has flown back from a performance in Atlanta, Georgia, that day – he could not miss this video shoot in east London because 'this is my ground; it's where I started out from'.

Interviews in Silvertown

Another respondent making his mark is Colin, a 24-year-old beatmaker and music producer: 'I make beats which can then be sung over by an MC or vocalist'. I interview him at the recording studio he has recently set up in Silvertown in the London borough of Newham. Colin, a confident but humble young man, describes the journey his father had made to finally arrive in east London in 1981: 'my dad came first, from India to Pakistan, onto Afghanistan then on a bus to Iran, he crossed the river to Dubai and then from Dubai to France, then here – crazy' (Colin, 24 – music producer – interviewed in 2011). Colin works with unsigned artists in the informal music economy, creates soundtracks for Bollywood films and tours with signed artists such as Wiley and Dizzee Rascal. He has also worked with independent recording artists such as Giggs, D Double E, Griminal and Ghetts. He is a trained classical musician – he plays the keyboards, tabla and harmonium. But despite achieving an A grade GCSE in Music in Year 9, he left secondary school in Newham with few qualifications. He had been drawn into the negative aspects of life in 'the ends' and had then become NEET. His east London was one where you 'grow up doing wrong things, thinking it's normal … on a good day, Joy, it's vibrant, on a bad day, it's red'. Colin tells me that his career break came from selling 8,000 copies of a mixtape he had produced for an unsigned urban artist.

From the interviews, it was evident that learning how to adapt cultural and creative practices to create and maintain sustainable businesses was key. For example, Sam was twenty-four years old, operating solely on a cash-in-hand basis, when I interviewed him in 2009. He had started out as an MC and was now a video director, creating videos for artists and performers wanting to showcase their work on Channel AKA and YouTube. Sam grew up in south London and described himself as 'the black Chris Martin' (from the band Coldplay). He explained how he soon learned that everyone wanted to be in front of the camera as a performer, whether they were skilled or not, but that there were few that could actually make a film of the proceedings:

> Alright, basically everybody wants to be a star, but there's loads of people wanna be artists, but there is not enough people doing the video directing, … and so when these people do come around it's in high demand, so I realised this and thought to myself, if I was just doing the Rap, yeah, I wouldn't get so far…. People didn't rate me as a rapper … I was a bit different from

everyone else, I believed in myself [created] mixtapes and I sold about 3,000 copies in the first year, enough money for me to invest in my first DVD and buy better studio equipment as well.

(Sam, 24 – video maker – interviewed in 2009)

Through trial and error and by watching the practice of others, Sam then learned how to film and edit music videos. He promoted his service through social media sites and by adding his logo and contact details to the videos that he had created and broadcast on YouTube.

By contrast, George, also twenty-four, was a graduate with a full-time managerial post in the corporate sector who had established a music production business working with a similar target market and customer base as Sam. He had also worked as a sound engineer for mainstream artists and recording studios. Nevertheless, George had to conduct his business activities alongside his day job: 'I have to do this on the side as well, but if there was a way of incorporating it to become my main job, I'd be more than happy'. George grew up in Beckton, an area in the south of the London borough of Newham, but had since moved out to a more affluent east London suburb because 'people leave you alone ... if I had children myself, I wouldn't like them growing up around there, you know. The people around you, they see what you've got, they see what you're striving to and they try to pull you back from it'.

Starting out: the new entrants

I also interviewed a number of young people trying to establish themselves in the urban music sector. Adam, a young man of east African heritage, was one of the new entrants to the field. He described himself as an '18-year-old rapper, upcoming artist, I write, produce, create instrumentals....'. The east London 'ends' Adam inhabited were 'a violent place, where ... crime pays, but I don't really watch that no more; if you've got a motive in life you can escape it, even if you still live here'. Adam had set up a recording studio in his bedroom at home to apply what he was learning on his music technology course at college. He was not a regular attender, going just often enough to get the information and knowledge that he needed to pursue his own endeavours. At the time of interview, he was working on his first EP 'trying to put my best work into my first project'. Adam left school at 16, but said he 'could have got kicked out earlier'. Music had helped him to drift away from the more negative activity that he was surrounded by. In his own words, 'I was one of them troubled kids'. During his interview, Adam was wearing a T-shirt with the name of his own brand emblazoned across the front.

Helen, a white English singer-songwriter also from east London, was a former stage school student who wanted to break into the music industry and felt that working with urban artists was a way in:

Yeah, well, I've already done theatre work since I was little, and at the moment I'm working pantomime and doing drama in college, studying

Theatre and Drama. Basically I've always done singing, ... and then later on, when I was about fourteen, my brothers, I've got two brothers, they was really into garage music and I started singing that just in my bedroom and I realised it really suited my voice, and then getting to about, say, a year ago I realised that, you know, the people that were singing the club music wasn't, you know, just aimed at black people.

(Helen, 18 – singer-songwriter – interviewed in 2009)

Helen described how she had tried to break into this market by creating 'specials' (a one-off recordings of popular tracks with the DJ's name sung throughout) for Hotsteppa, a Radio 1Xtra DJ, and Marcus Nasty, a pirate radio and club DJ. However, Helen's experience of east London differed to that of Adam and Harvey:

You know, it's [east London area] a lovely area, you're always meeting people, I talk to people from America or South Africa or Pakistan then they come to live here for a few months and then moving on, you know ... a worldly place to live in, with all these opportunities.

(Helen, 18 – singer-songwriter – interviewed in 2009)

In these two different geographical settings, both Adam and Helen had a clear sense of their skills and talents. It was this that motivated them to seek ways to enter the urban music economy.

Artist-entrepreneurs in their social context

Far from operating in a vacuum, entrepreneurship is a social phenomenon anchored within a socio-cultural context (Drakopoulou Dodd and Anderson 2007; Thornton *et al.* 2011). Social capital, in terms of concrete resources such as editing and production skills and tangible resources such as feedback, positive regard and appreciation, are gained from working in this sector (Thornton *et al.* 2011). Artist-entrepreneurs in the urban music economy challenge the accepted notion of the entrepreneur by undertaking activity clearly rooted in their social and cultural circumstance but extending that to the wider world. These artist-entrepreneurs are firmly located in their inner-city environs and therefore economic capital is scarce. In Figure 3.1, I have illustrated the inputs and influences that impact on becoming an artist-entrepreneur. Once artist-entrepreneurs have scanned the horizon and have an awareness of the limited opportunities available, they then draw on their creative and/or technical skills to carve out a niche for themselves. They can hone these skills through practicing, observing other 'old hands' and mentoring. They also have access to technology, social media, online broadcasting and specialised digital TV channels, where they can disseminate their creative output directly to their audience and receive feedback. The urban music economy therefore creates an environment in which artist-entrepreneurs can learn from each other. This is enhanced by accessible

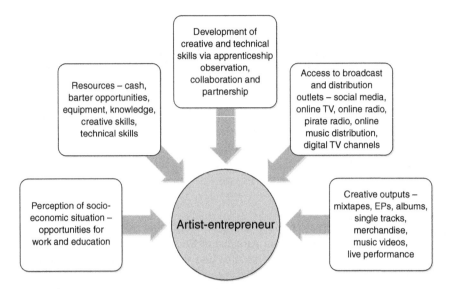

Figure 3.1 Becoming an artist-entrepreneur in the urban music economy.

communication and social media, which enable a cross-fertilisation not just of creative ideas, but of business ideas also. The products developed include mixtapes – now essentially a collection of tracks for download rather than a physical product – as well as single tracks and associated merchandise such as clothing.

When few resources are available, being able to pool skills and knowledge means that your track, and the accompanying video, will be more likely to come to fruition. For example, an MC needs a producer to mix the track, and needs a beat to rhyme over, so there are multiple actors and stakeholders in the creation and distribution of a piece of work. These artist-entrepreneurs take from and give back to the social realm in terms of material for their creative output and as source of relevant and readily available skills (Drakopoulou Dodd and Anderson 2007). My informants are an integral part of their social and economic situation and, for the most part, these circumstances have less to offer in terms of employment and opportunity. Some of the participants in this economy learned by doing; others became conversant by watching others and taking their inspiration from them. This was possible in part because of the creative grime clusters that developed on council estates like Meridian in Tottenham (in north London) and on street corners like Greengate in Plaistow (in east London), but also because of advances in technology such as the Internet and social media, which allowed this creative practice to become highly visible.

Conclusion

On the whole, artist-entrepreneurs in the urban music economy remain invisible. This may be because they belong to an ethnically coded, stigmatised community: they are young, black and poor (Wacquant 2007). It may also be because if they are categorised as NEET and therefore, ostensibly, not in education, employment or training, they are classified by what they are *not* doing. Therefore what they *are* doing is rarely recorded. The challenge for young people from these and other impoverished areas is to establish themselves in a world that is closed off to them, particularly if they are placed in a NEET category and have limited access to good quality, paid work.

I have foregrounded the working lives of young people in the urban music economy, who draw on their passion for music to make meaningful work for themselves and others in an environment where opportunities are scarce. Although 'the ends' remain a site of repressive practices where, according to Victor, the drug dealers are the 'success stories' and, in George's words, 'people try and pull you back', these neighbourhoods also offer comfort, kinship and the raw materials for an innovative musical practice that allows for self-employment and enterprise.

At the same time, regenerated cities, or districts of cities, benefit some (usually the middle classes) but damage others (usually those who are already at a disadvantage) (Rosler 2011). In the discussion regarding creative clusters and creative cities in the east end of London what is often being talked about is the presence of new white middle-class residents (Pratt 2009; Mayor of London 2010). Little reference is made to the existing creative practice of grime artists when expounding the virtues and economic relevance of the innovative hubs in Shoreditch and Hoxton. The powers that be try to hang on to working-class 'authenticity' and 'grit' while eradicating it from its places of origin, such as inner-city east London (Zukin 2010).

The hierarchy of achievement negates and obscures the activities and contributions of the urban poor. According to a recent University of Warwick report (Neelands *et al.* 2015), the cultural and creative industries workforce continues to be overwhelmingly white and middle class and 'we face a situation in which the voices, experiences and talents of the UK's population as a whole are not being expressed, represented or developed within the Cultural and Creative Industries'. Yet I have shown that, in plain sight, young people from poor communities create work with very little capital. This work covers a broad range in the creative and cultural sector – music, film, cultural events, radio and video – and allows them to develop skills, knowledge and expertise.

Notes

1 The London 2012 Olympics promised a legacy of a healthier nation, affordable homes and increased job opportunities in the host boroughs of Newham, Hackney, Greenwich, Tower Hamlets and Waltham Forest.
2 Joint enterprise is a 300-year-old law to ensure the sharing of responsibility for a crime, not only among those that participated, but also including those that were present. This

can mean mandatory life sentences for fringe or secondary participants in serious crimes such as murder. The Supreme Court is currently reviewing the doctrine.
3 The Newham Show is an annual two-day summer event in the London borough of Newham showcasing local talent.
4 In the early days, sound systems would bring their equipment to each venue they played at. Equipment included speakers, cables and record boxes, as well as the decks. A 'box boy' helped to move the equipment from the van to the venue and back again.
5 This is an English and Welsh football chant that has been adapted for other crowd occasions, the usual response to which is 'oi, oi, oi'.
6 Hood videos usually require groups of young men (sometimes women) to populate the background scenes.
7 'Freestyling' is an impromptu or unplanned performance.

References

Aldridge, H., Barry Born, T. Tinson, A. MacInnes, T., 2015. *London's poverty profile 2015*, London, UK: New Policy Institute.
Allen, M. and Ainley, P., 2007. *Education make you fick, innit?: What's gone wrong in England's schools, colleges and universities and how to start putting it right*, London, UK: Tufnell Press.
Anderson, A.R. and Warren, L., 2011. The entrepreneur as hero and jester: Enacting the entrepreneurial discourse. *International Small Business Journal*, 29(6), pp. 589–609.
AndyManch, 2011. *Cocoa Tea, Home T & Shabba Ranks – Pirates' Anthem*. Available at: www.youtube.com/watch?v=6shUOKb4Md4&feature=youtube_gdata_player [accessed 10 November 2013].
Bainbridge, L. and Browne, A., 2010. *Generation Neet*, York: Report for Children and Young People Now Magazine.
Ball, J., Milmo, D. and Ferguson, B., 2012. Half of UK's young black males are unemployed. *Guardian*. Available at: www.guardian.co.uk/society/2012/mar/09/half-uk-young-black-men-unemployed [accessed 12 April 2012].
BBC London, 2008. Are the Olympic boroughs on track? Available at: www.bbc.co.uk/london/content/articles/2008/08/18/five_boroughs_progress_feature.shtml [accessed 13 November 2013].
Bingham, J., 2013. White boys 'the problem' for Britain's schools, says government aide. *Telegraph*. Available at: www.telegraph.co.uk/education/educationnews/10375879/White-boys-the-problem-for-Britains-schools-says-Government-aide.html [accessed 19 October 2013].
Blanden, J. and Machin, S., 2007. *Recent changes in intergenerational mobility in Britain*, London, UK: Sutton Trust.
chocdip, 2006. *Crazy Titch merkin da cab driver*. Available at: www.youtube.com/watch?v=xxjnuHlTRzM&feature=youtube_gdata_player [accessed 20 December 2010].
Clifton, J. and Cook, W., 2012. *A long division: Closing the attainment gap in England's secondary schools*, London: IPPR.
Communities and Local Government, 2009. Black role models: Which messages work? Available at: http://communities.gov.uk/publications/communities/reachmessages [accessed 15 September 2010].
Cunningham, A., 2012. NEETs: A lost generation. *Total Politics*. Available at: www.total-politics.com/articles/344172/neets-a-lost-generation.thtml [accessed 26 January 2013].
Drakopoulou Dodd, S. and Anderson, A.R., 2007. Mumpsimus and the mything of the individualistic entrepreneur. *International Small Business Journal*, 25(4), pp. 341–360.

Earle, R., 2011. Boys' zone stories: Perspectives from a young men's prison. *Criminology and Criminal Justice*, 11(2), pp. 129–143.

Elkes, N., 2013. Almost half of children below poverty line in Nechells and Sparkbrook. *Birminghammail*. Available at: www.birminghammail.co.uk/news/local-news/half-children-below-poverty-line-1335844 [accessed 22 June 2013].

Furlong, A. and Cartmel, F., 2007. *Young people and social change new perspectives*, Maidenhead: McGraw-Hill/Open University Press.

Gilroy, P., 1996. *The Black Atlantic*, London: Verso.

Gunter, A., 2010. *Growing up bad? Black youth, road culture and badness in an east London neighbourhood*, London, UK: Tufnell Press.

Hill-Collins, P., 2006. New commodities, new consumers: Selling blackness in a global marketplace. *Ethnicities*, 6(3), pp. 297–317.

Hills, J., 2010. National equality panel. Available at: www.equalities.gov.uk/national_equality_panel.aspx [accessed 20 December 2010].

Leitch, L., 2006. Leitch review of skills: Prosperity for all in the global economy: World-class skills. *HM Treasury*.

London Borough of Hackney, 2005. Hackney local improvement plan.

London Borough of Newham, 2005. Newham local implementation plan.

London Borough of Tower Hamlets, 2005. Tower Hamlets local implementation plan.

Mac an Ghaill, M., 1996. *Understanding masculinities: Social relations and cultural arenas*, Buckingham, UK: Open University.

MacRury, I. and Poynter, G., 2009. *London's Olympic legacy*, University of East London: London East Research Institute.

Mayor of London, 2010. *Cultural metropolis: The mayor's cultural strategy: 2012 and Beyond*, London: GLA.

Murray, S. and Gayle, V., 2012. *Youth transitions*, University of Stirling.

Neelands, J., Belfiore, E., Firth, C., Hart, N., Perrin, L., Brock, S., Holdaway, D. and Woddis, J., 2015. *Enriching Britain: Culture, creativity and growth*, University of Warwick.

Oliver, W., 2006. 'The streets': An alternative black male socialization institution. *Journal of Black Studies*, 36(6), pp. 918–937.

Pickernell, D., Senyard, J., Jones, P., Packham, G. and Ramsey, E., 2013. New and young firms: Entrepreneurship policy and the role of government: Evidence from the Federation of Small Businesses survey. *Journal of Small Business and Enterprise Development*, 20(2), pp. 358–382.

Pratt, A.C., 2009. Urban regeneration: From the arts 'feel good' factor to the cultural economy: A case study of Hoxton. *Urban Studies*, 46(5–6), pp. 1041–1061.

Randhawa, K., 2013. Children in Tower Hamlets are poorest in UK with 42 per cent living below breadline. *The Evening Standard*. Available at: www.standard.co.uk/news/london/children-in-tower-hamlets-are-poorest-in-uk-with-42-per-cent-living-below-breadline-8502616.html [accessed 22 June 2013].

Reynolds, T., 2013. 'Them and us': 'Black neighbourhoods' as a social capital resource among black youths living in inner-city London. *Urban Studies*, 50(3), pp. 484–498.

Rosler, M., 2011. Culture class: Art, creativity, urbanism, Part II. Available at: www.e-flux.com/journal/culture-class-art-creativity-urbanism-part-ii/ [accessed 21 June 2013].

Shepherd, J., 2010. Poor literacy and maths skills leave teenagers ill-equipped. *Guardian*. Available at: www.guardian.co.uk/education/2010/may/07/poor-literacy-numeracy [accessed 20 December 2010].

Shildrick, T., MacDonald, R., Webster, C. and Garthwaite, K., 2010. The low-pay, no-pay cycle: Understanding recurrent poverty, London, UK: Joseph Rowntree Foundation.

Skidmore, C., 2008. Boys: A school report. London: Bow Group.

Taylor, M., 2005. Many school-leavers lack basic skills, admits education head. *Guardian*. Available at: www.guardian.co.uk/uk/2005/oct/13/schools.politics [accessed 20 December 2010].

Thornton, P.H., Ribeiro-Soriano, D. and Urbano, D., 2011. Socio-cultural factors and entrepreneurial activity: An overview. *International Small Business Journal*, 29(2), pp. 105–118.

Tomlinson, S., 2005. *Education in a post-welfare society*, 2nd edn, Maidenhead, UK: Open University Press.

Wacquant, L., 2007. *Urban outcasts: A comparative sociology of advanced marginality*, Cambridge, UK: Polity.

Willemse, N. and de Beer, P., 2012. Three worlds of educational welfare states? A comparative study of higher education systems across welfare states. *Journal of European Social Policy*, 22(2), pp. 105–117.

Zukin, S., 2010. *Naked city: The death and life of authentic urban places*, Oxford and New York: Oxford University Press.

4   Business studies from 'the ends'

Learning the rules of the game

> I've made money, but not enough, and not in a sensible way, not something that I
> could honestly say yes, 'cos right now it's more like side money. So I want some-
> thing in a solid way, if I get residency, then I've got set money coming in. If I get
> two or three, then it's like a regular income, so that's what I'm aiming for.
>
> (James, 25 – club and pirate radio DJ – interviewed in 2008)

Introduction

In a landscape where entry-level jobs suitable for young people have been all but
eradicated and youth unemployment remains high (Furlong and Cartmel 2007;
Murray and Gayle 2012), I have identified young people who have moved in and
out of the NEET category to become artist-entrepreneurs and business owners.
These individuals have established businesses that have enabled them to move
beyond the boundaries of their inner-city environments to create meaningful
work for themselves and others. They have developed, through informal learning, the necessary skills, knowledge and capabilities to be legitimate players in
the urban music economy.

Because a key focus of this book is the extent of entrepreneurship within the
urban music economy, it is crucial to consider the complexities and intercon-
nectedness of these business strands. The urban music economy is a complex
fabric containing a multiplicity of roles and practitioners operating within and
across the sector as artists and as entrepreneurs. In this chapter, I have used a
narrative approach to provide an enhanced reading of what motivates young
people from impoverished backgrounds to establish their own business and the
process by which they become enterprising individuals (Johansson 2004).

The participants in this research project form part of a wider discourse that
renders young black men in particular as both troubled and troublesome. The
majority of the informants in this book emerge from this social constituency.
While many had at some point been classified as NEET, all were active agents in
the urban music economy. They had, on the whole, learned the rules of the game
by immersing themselves in the setting, observing others, getting feedback and
through trial and error. Gifts of time, equipment or other resources were an
invaluable contribution to business start-up. But essentially, what underpins the

practice is the participants' desire to share their creativity with the widest possible audience.

Four decades ago, in the pre-Internet days, urban music events were publicised through flyers in community settings, record shops and barbershops. Performers relied on these mainly word-of-mouth pursuits to promote their public image and forthcoming activities. Advances in technology have meant that it has become less costly to record music and to produce music videos. The proliferation in digital TV channels has enabled a flow to and from online TV channels and a wide dissemination of urban music on a local and national level. From the simple act of searching for a performing name on Google, it is possible to observe how the utilisation of Web 2.0 technology has enabled young people in the urban music economy to establish an online presence and disseminate their creative output.

Music videos, shot cheaply and uploaded on YouTube and then promoted via social media, support the creation of an online persona as an MC, DJ, beatmaker, producer or entrepreneur. On YouTube generally, and on niche online channels such as SBTV, Linkup TV and GRM Daily, in particular, young people from impoverished backgrounds use performance to construct identities that showcase and highlight excellence, innovation, oratory and humour. Nevertheless, this transition into an online persona has not been without its challenges.

My informants expressed that they had little use for what they had learned at school. Indeed, learning about 'old-school guys' like Pavarotti bore no relevance to their planned or actual career in the music industry. The business component of the creative practice is in evidence throughout, from DJs paying subscriptions to play on pirate radio to the filming of low-cost music videos. In the final part of the chapter, I explore the themes of collaborative practice, entry points into the business world and getting by, by drawing on the operations of four key businesses in the urban music sector.

The urban music economy in evidence

At its heart, economics is about the invisible hand of supply and demand. It is concerned with the decisions that people make and the impact those choices have on wider society. The informal economy has been defined as those involved in the process of producing goods and services that are legal but not registered for tax and employment law purposes (see Gerxhani 2004; Chen 2007, p. 1; Llanes and Barbour 2007, p. 12). However, the informal/formal distinction is used here as an heuristic device, as a way to explore how the urban music economy manifests itself; the activities do not fall easily into one category or the other. The goods and services traditionally identified as likely to occur in the informal sector are personal services such as hairdressing and catering, but as I show throughout the book, the urban music sector is also a significant economic area.

The urban music economy operates at a formal and informal level. Its practitioners acquire the necessary skills and knowledge to create businesses and generate self-employment. Grime music and its by-products can therefore be used as a tool to discover how this economy operates and who participates in it. Although some of the respondents are not working within this music genre per se, they do occupy positions within the same economic ecology, such as in pirate radio stations, music videos and nightclubs.

All of my informants participated in the informal music economy while having a business or artistic reach into the formal sector. This informal music economy may appear, at a first glance, to be a chaotic collection of individuals creating a niche genre of music for a very specific urban audience. It may also seem to be invisible or inaccessible to everday, ordinary folk. This is not the case. Of the forty people that I interviewed, twenty-two had a booking agent or a manager, or both. Two of my informants, George and Diane, acted as agents for others. The events I attended were subject to all of the usual health and safety and licensing regulations. If it was a ticketed event, tickets could be bought online, in retail outlets or from the promoter. Only the cultural seminars operated on a strictly cash-at-the-door basis. The urban music economy is not an unregulated sector. If, as Will Straw states in the *Club Cultures Reader*, 'DJing is now a proper job' (Redhead *et al.* 1998, p. 161), then the same can be said for being an MC or an event promoter.

The informal economy

The informal economy involves undertaking the production of legal goods and services by individuals who are not registered for tax and other legislative requirements, including employment relationships that are cash-in-hand or off-the-books. During the primary research phase it became apparent that the urban music economy has a compelling role because it offers a variety of products and services. Some authors consider the informal economy an intrinsic part of the socio-economic landscape in the developed world, including the UK (Grabiner 2000; Losby *et al.* 2002; Venkatesh 2002; Williams 2006; Llanes and Barbour 2007). Others suggest that within the informal sector there are those that could work officially but choose not to for a number of reasons, including formally paid employees who work 'on the side' (Tanzi 1999; Grabiner 2000; Schneider 2004; Williams 2006). This was indeed true for some of my informants.

The prevailing notion is that the formal and informal sectors are separate markets, the former highly regulated and driven by enterprising individuals; the latter occupied by the marginal activities of the less educated western poor (Tanzi 1999; Grabiner 2000; Williams 2006, p. 31). Nevertheless, it can also be argued that rather than becoming less significant in developed societies, the informal economy is here to stay and presents itself in innovative ways and novel places such as the urban music economy (Chen 2007, p. 7). Even without a concrete definition of what or who is an entrepreneur, their actions and decisions can kick-start the economy and generate wealth (Schoof 2006; Chell 2007; Pickernell *et al.* 2013). But, perhaps with the recent exception of Jamal Edwards and SBTV, little attention has been paid to the artist-entrepreneur in the urban music economy (Edwards 2013; Smale 2013). Consider these comments made by Marcelli, Pastor and Joussart: 'Selling oranges in a grocery store is a formal economic activity. Selling them on a highway exit ramp in Los Angeles County to passing motorists is an informal activity' (cited in Losby *et al.* 2002, p. 5). This view suggests that perhaps the grocery store will always be in the same place and that the person who sells the oranges in the store will have all of the required permissions. On the other hand, the unregulated seller, positioned on the highway exit ramp, might be in different location tomorrow; also there is no guarantee about the quality of the product or the validity of the seller (does the informal orange seller have a contract of employment?). In reality, though, it is possible that the grocery store uses 'cash-in-hand' labour and that the grocery store owner does not pay all of the necessary taxes.

The discussion regarding the informal urban music sector often centres on ethnicity and underachievement, underpinned by the negative impact of aggressive behaviour and violent lyrics in what is often erroneously termed 'rap music'. Recent studies have pointed out that research into African-Caribbean youth has been largely confined to the problematic of young black men, namely a socio-political concern about rioting, knife crime, gun crime and gangs (Gunter 2010). This is underpinned by the use of the hypermasculinity of the scene as evidence of violence and negativity and augments a categorisation of young black men as powerless and marginalised (Keyes 2004; Collinson 2006; Muir 2006; Wolfson 2013). Yet this same community is over-represented both as victims and as perpetrators of violent crime (Rose 2008; Stickler 2008). For example, in his investigation into 'Britain's gang culture' John Heale retells the story of the escalating incidents between two musicians from east London, which eventually resulted in a murder, and accepts that the lyrics are a key factor in the subsequent crime (Heale 2008, p. 1). The incident, reported in 2006, relates to Carl Dobson, also known as grime MC Crazy Titch, who was jailed for thirty years for his involvement in the shooting of a music producer. The *Guardian* reported that the fatal incident started with a row over song lyrics deemed by Crazy Titch to denigrate him and his brother.

Entrepreneurship: the social and cultural context

Since the 1980s, the pursuit of enterprise has been assumed to provide a solution to a profusion of social and economic problems including youth unemployment. Entrepreneurship is seen to be the process by which the economy as a whole moves forward. It disrupts the equilibrium of the market (through innovation and new combinations) and creates movement. It is therefore at the root of economic improvement and is seen to be the key to economic growth, productivity and the diffusion of knowledge.

It has been argued that there is a correlation between the number of entrepreneurs and the growth rate of the economy, and indeed the creation of new firms is seen as a driving force for economic growth (Low and MacMillan 1988; Schumpeter 1994; Baumol 1996; Stevenson and Jarillo 2007). Furthermore, enterprise culture is posited as an alternative to a culture of dependency, and in the UK over the last fifteen years there has been a rise in self-employment and new, small firms (Macdonald *et al.* 2013). In dense urban settings such as inner-city east London, enterprise generates opportunities for growth and employment. Nevertheless, although the concept of entrepreneurship can appear to be undefined, and the entrepreneurial process complex and often beyond reach, entrepreneurs are real people from existent social and cultural contexts, and yet this is often overlooked. Much of the literature on entrepreneurship is focused on the usually heroic individual and their personal traits and individual activities (Cunningham and Lischeron 1991; Carland *et al.* 2002; Anderson *et al.* 2009). However, some authors suggest that not enough attention is has been given to the social and cultural context from which entrepreneurs emerge (Drakopoulou Dodd and Anderson 2007). The individuals who participate in the urban music economy were from, on the whole, poor socio-economic backgrounds. This situation may limit their hopes and aspirations for paid employment, but this economy allows them to create new identities and opportunities. The artist-entrepreneur I have identified in the urban music economy has some similarities with the concept of barefoot economics developed by Manfred Max-Neef, who argued that the barefoot entrepreneur is a person with few resources who enriches themselves through the creation of work while operating at the periphery of the economy (Imas *et al.* 2012). Where the artist-entrepreneur differs is that they operate, largely unseen, not at the margins but at the heart of the economy within a complex network of collaboration and partnership.

For my informants, their social and cultural context was, on the whole, one of underachievement and a lack of interest in formal education underpinned by a passion for their particular craft. This ability was honed by the acquisition of the relevant skills and knowledge, usually through mentoring, shadowing and trial and error. An exception to this was Gillian, a 27-year-old graduate of Caribbean heritage who I interviewed in Hoxton in 2011. She had grown up in Manchester Moss Side and had recently set up her own limited company in east London. Gillian provided services as a make-up artist-stylist for photo shoots and music video shoots. She told me she had been networking and shadowing for five years to acquire the requisite knowledge and skills. She was now working with corporate clients such as Adidas, as well as urban artists: 'I've worked with ... most of them, really, ... Firecamp, Kano, Ghetts, Ny, Mz Bratt, Wiley, Scorcher, Wretch 32'. A family member's giving her a camera when she was fifteen years old was the start of Fiona's interest in film-making. Fiona said that she had been a music video director for eight years, since she was sixteen years old, when:

> I wrote to every production company, I had a Saturday job [in a newsagents] and I would look though the magazines to find contacts ... eventually I found a production company that would take me on as a runner ... on the set of a music video I realised that for a small amount of time [you could be] taken into the world that belongs to the artist.
>
> (Fiona, 24 – music video director – interviewed in 2011)

This propelled her into the world of music video production at a time when urban music artists needed inexpensive videos to promote their artistic output on fledgling online TV broadcasters such as SBTV on YouTube and Channel AKA, the digital TV channel.

In the urban music economy, the concept of the 'bring in' is key; in other words, collaboration is actively sought and expected. This partnership approach enables the establishment of creative clusters where ideas and resources can be shared, thus stimulating innovation and novel combinations. These entrepreneurs understand their target market and recognise that their customers do not have high levels of disposable income; therefore, some products and services are provided free or at low cost. The free music download or mixtape for promotional purposes is a central feature of the supply side of the urban music economy.

Being NEET excludes, or positions you further from, the labour market; self-employment and enterprise can be a way to combat this. Although their employment choices were curtailed and constrained by circumstance because they originated from, and were located in, areas of high unemployment and low social mobility, my informants wanted their creativity to be viewed by the widest possible audience and to provide an opportunity to launch them into the world of paid work (White 2014). This is particularly germane for those who inhabit a world in which paid employment offered by an external organisation is scarce. As James, a DJ, told me in an early interview in 2008:

> you have to make yourself like a brand. It's not just like being a DJ it's like you have to work it kind of thing. It's like a game. You have to put yourself about, put CDs out, marketing basically ... if you get that right then you can be big, people will look for you. That's what I want to do, push myself more on the marketing side of it cos it's all good being good at all that but if no one gets to hear you, it don't matter.
>
> (James, 25 – internet and radio DJ – interviewed in 2008)

Since that interview, James has established a sustainable enterprise, an online radio station that comprises DJs who broadcast from around the world, including San Francisco, Toronto and Rome. The business model for his radio station emulates the pirate radio set-up where James learned his craft, in that budding DJs pay for the opportunity to broadcast. Therefore this business also acts as a training ground and provides a possibility for entry into wider work opportunities (White 2014). Another of my informants was Edward, who wanted to build his grime crew into a business organisation where everyone got paid – 'no dodginess'. At the time of writing he has done just that, setting up a limited company and trademarking his clothing brand. Another informant, Fiona, 'saw the world in pictures' and used her passion for music to create her own employment in a male dominated environment. Since she left school at the age of sixteen with few qualifications, Fiona has been making a living as a music video director. Brian, a 40-year-old van driver, wanted to: 'Get my own label, make my own music, get into production', based on what he had seen others do. He also viewed it as a natural career progression from being a DJ.

Most people start out in business doing what they love and subsequently find a way to get paid for it (Williams 2006; Albert and Couture 2013). In *The Hidden Enterprise Culture*, Williams reveals that the majority of those working off the books are not in a stereotypical 'sweatshop' environment but participating in enterprise on a self-employed basis. While the definition of entrepreneurship remains elusive, Williams is able to identify the individual traits attributed to entrepreneurs. These attributes include the need for independence, the need for achievement and the ability to take risks and live with uncertainty, as well as being innovative and self-motivated (2006, p. 18). These characteristics are clearly demonstrated by my informants.

In the *English Localities Survey* (cited in Williams 2006), three types of 'autonomous underground worker' are identified: the underground micro-entrepreneur, who starts up a fledgling business as a short-term risk-taking strategy to test out or establish themselves (these workers are either in employment or 'economically inactive' or NEET); the established 'off-the-books' self-employed worker, who is in formal employment while conducting self-employed work 'off-the-books' (such as my informant George, who ran his music production company alongside his paid employment in the corporate sector); and finally the 'off-the-books' social entrepreneur, who carries out one-off tasks or takes cash for favours (Williams 2006, p. 68). Participating in this way appears to be a short-term strategy (whether this is through choice or necessity is a moot point). Many of my informants started their self-employment or business activity because that was the only way they could undertake the work they desired. In the wider creative economy, jobs as radio presenters and music video directors are at a premium. Those with social and economic capital can participate in internships as a means for entry into the sector; however, this is difficult for those from marginalised communities, particularly if they have limited academic qualifications. Therefore, although people might choose this option because it provides autonomy, flexibility, freedom and independence, they make this choice due to certain 'push' factors, such as unemployment, entrenched joblessness and economic adversity. Furthermore, the formal sector now operates with increasingly informal and unstable work patterns, such as fixed and zero-hours contracts, and workers who do participate in the formal sector are often no better off financially (Macdonald *et al.* 2013).

In the UK, grime and subsequent urban music genres came of age in the YouTube era, that is, from 2005 onwards. Therefore, what in previous times would have been a highly localised practice was now immediately visible to other artists as well as fans, and could elicit an instantaneous response. Here, in this urban music economy, we have the dynamics of young white working-class communities juxtaposed in physical proximity with those of Caribbean and African descent. This, in turn, creates a genre that exposes the positive externalities of affordable technology and widened access to publication and broadcast. In an era in which the fear of the impact of the free music download is palpable, increased opportunities for live and recorded performance become available through the activities of these artist-entrepreneurs.

One key distribution and dissemination method for practitioners in the urban music economy is Channel AKA. Channel AKA, a digital television station, has been in existence since 2003. It originally started life as a station broadcasting rock and other popular music genres. It enables artists and aspiring artists to broadcast their videos for a nominal fee. In theory, for a small amount of money, a budding artist in the urban music economy may have a music video aired nationwide. This video can also cross over, and if MTV Base or another mainstream channel takes it up, it can gain national recognition and perhaps monetary success as well as personal achievement. Channel AKA offers grime artists accessible broadcasting, but because it is monitored and regulated by Ofcom (Ofcom 2013),[1] the communications regulator that regulates the TV and radio sectors, rules apply. These rules impose order and conformity, and as the Channel AKA identity established itself, it broadcast less 'road'[2] videos than when it was known as Channel U.

For these artists, rules notwithstanding,[3] Channel AKA offers an opportunity for visibility (Channel AKA 2013). The compulsion to perform is strong; so technology is mastered, and bartering and exchange take place to raise the capital to produce a video that meets the criteria. From its original target audience, Channel AKA has emerged as a prime arena in which urban music artists can gain prominence and recognition. Since its inception Dizzee Rascal, Kano, Skepta, Tinchy Stryder, Tinie Tempah and Wiley, for example, have come to national attention.

There is a flow to and from Channel AKA and YouTube, the video sharing website established in 2005. Formally produced music videos can be aired on Channel AKA and shared on YouTube. The 'collection of video pebbles' that constitutes YouTube (Leadbeater 2009, p. xvii) requires relatively few permissions, enabling artists to promote themselves directly to a potential fan base. A video on YouTube with a high number of views can also generate advertising revenue (Cunningham 2012). Viewers can comment or give feedback on the performance, and the artist can engage in direct dialogue with their audience. Cultural production requires a continuous supply of people to do the work, and cultural consumption needs a steady creation of new markets (Hill Collins 2006, p. 301). Rather than, as Paul Gilroy feared, the technological revolution in music making leading to a lessening in the amount of public performance (Gilroy 1993, p. 5), YouTube and Channel AKA have provided a platform for a new market, in which urban artists can be both producers and users of music products.

Business studies: learning to be enterprising

If, as Malcolm Tight asserts, learning is like breathing and it is something we do all the time, it is worth exploring the process by which the participants in this sector learn to do business (Dennick 2008). The debate about what education is for continues unabated. Indeed, these artist-entrepreneurs have grown up and been schooled in a time of what Tomlinson refers to as constant flurry policymaking, which saw one or more Education Acts passed every year in the period from 1988 to 1994 (Tomlinson 2005). Perhaps, then, it is no wonder that Rogers is convinced that learning has been transformed into a 'dull, mind numbing experience' (1983, cited in Dennick 2008, p. 68), or that the formal learning experience for many of my informants was at best a hindrance or of little relevance.

Ian is a DJ. When I interviewed him in 2008 he was working on a cash-in-hand basis in clubs and using his stints on pirate radio to raise awareness of his work. Since then, he has secured a regular weekly radio show with a licensed broadcaster:

> Yeah, they didn't really teach me anything too tough, about like mixing or anything, so I sorted it out all myself. But yeah, they could have taught us a bit more about music cos, really and truly it was just about the old-school guys and stuff.... Like Pavarotti and stuff, them sort of people, they don't really relate to me.
>
> (Ian, 22 – club and radio DJ – interviewed in 2008)

For Quentin, now a vocalist/MC/host, 'college ... not good, spent all day smoking weed and chasing girls, more social than study'. Edward, a 20-year-old grime MC and former DJ, reflected on his time at secondary school (he ended up in a pupil referral unit):

> 'Cos obviously, because of my behaviour in school I couldn't gain qualifications and after that, that was when I started in the music industry ... I was excluded a few times for things ... just immature behaviour, just things like not paying attention and constantly leaving my seat, just childish things really, which I regret up to this day.

Charlotte was a few months in to her career as a model, working for a north London model agency. This agency had started out providing models for urban music videos, but now focused on providing models for the fashion industry:

> It's not that I wanted to be a legal secretary, but when I left school I didn't know what I wanted to do, so my mum said that it was a good career, like the money's good so you can get, like, a qualification for it. You can just fall back on to it. But I've always wanted to be a model; I've never really been into studying and things like that.
> JW: So what did you learn at school which is useful to you now?
> Nothing
> JW: Nothing?
> No, honestly I don't think [so], I think that school's good because you learn lots of social skills, you know, and how to interact with people, but actual things you learn in lessons, like, no I don't really use them, it's just like, I don't think that me going to school proves anything.
>
> (Charlotte, 18 – model – interviewed in 2008)

However, although some informants deemed school to be of little or no import-ance, specific college courses targeted at practical aspects of the music industry were felt to be useful:

> So because of that, because I done music business in college, that really helped, and I'd advise any girl or guy who wants to do their own under-ground music and work their way up to get commercial, to make sure they know the foundations of it, or otherwise people walk all over you.
>
> (Helen, 18 – singer-songwriter – interviewed in 2009)

As in other occupational and industrial sectors, starting a business in the urban music economy is often a by-product of a hobby or interest. For example, Jamal Edwards started his company, SBTV, as an outlet for his interest in making videos for the grime music he loved. By first establishing a YouTube partnership advert-ising deal[4] and then achieving contracts with other companies such as Virgin Unite, Edwards has turned SBTV into a global brand (Edwards 2013, p. 151; Smale 2013). This is one well-documented example of learning how to create an enterprise in a setting that traditionally has little value except as a source of new talent for the recording industry. Sizeable numbers of young people who have been ill served by formal education participate in the urban music economy. Becoming an artist-entrepreneur in the urban music economy is experiential: the rules of the game are learned by observing, carrying out the activity and getting feedback.

At the other end of the scale from Jamal Edwards, my informant Fred has always occupied an unstable position at the margins of the economy. Apart from a brief placement on a youth training scheme in his early teenage years, he has rarely participated in formal paid employment. At the time of the interview, Fred was a 40-year-old man of Caribbean heritage who had inhabited the NEET cat-egory for most of his adult life. Fred operates in different guises and in a number of spheres: as a voice-over artist for pirate radio, a radio presenter, a teacher and an event promoter. At my first visit, Fred was in pirate radio DJ mode. He had learned his craft by working his way up through a key north London sound system in the 1980s. In his own words, he had been a 'pioneer, and a whizz kid … we paved the way for these young guys now'. At a visit to the radio station I observed Fred at work:

> It is a cold Saturday morning in mid January. I'm waiting in my car on the corner of a main road in east London (London Borough of Tower Hamlets). I have arranged to meet a friend who will take me to meet Fred. Fred has a Saturday morning talk show on a pirate radio station that broadcasts throughout north and east London.
>
> Fred has agreed that I can sit in while he broadcasts his show. I meet up with my friend and he directs me to the location – a semi occupied light industrial building. There is a small car park where we leave the car. Once we arrive, my friend calls Fred on his personal mobile (radio station has its own mobile number).

Fred says it's ok to come up, so we get out of the car and walk to a reinforced steel gate. We walk up three flights of concrete steps. We pass some other occupied rooms on the way – the doors are labelled with various business names – including a cable TV channel. There is one toilet, with no chain, and no door.

We arrive at the room that the radio station operates from. It is about 6' by 8' maximum. It is very cold in the room. Fred, dressed in a tracksuit, baseball cap and a bulky bomber jacket, greets us, indicates for us to come in and sit down while he carries on lining up the next few tracks to be played. While we wait – I look at his equipment, the tools of his trade; pc, large microphone, decks, old Nokia3310 mobile phone, cigarettes, rolling papers, a blue coloured energy drink, four cheese rolls and a Toblerone chocolate bar. There is a tall stool for the DJ, two small folding chairs (for guests), Saturday's edition of the Times newspaper and a black dustbin bag. The room has a security gate, the key to the gate is attached by a metal chain to the wall.

Fred is in full flow – playing a selection of music and indicating the discussion/themes for today's show. For this week only, he explains to the listeners, he will cover the 9 a.m.–12 p.m. instead of his usual slot. Fred is moving gracefully in the small, tight space; he does not bump into anything. He expertly cues the music while taking requests, reading out texts, working his way through the cheese rolls, and the cigarettes.

For this week's show the theme is business and Fred invites people to discuss economic power – especially for the black community. One listener, however, texts in to ask about the devil – Fred reassures her and his other listeners that this issue will be addressed in next week's show. Throughout the hour – ad breaks are played – forthcoming events, community activities and raves. Fred moves easily from discussion to music (soul, R & B, reggae) and back again. Although Fred keeps telling his listeners that the 'phone lines are blowing up' in response to the questions he is posing about black business, in fact the phone rings only once. It is the owner of the radio station, who calls in to congratulate on the content and to ask for the mic to be turned up a little louder.

The walls in the room are covered in marketing and teaching materials. There are posters exhorting the teachings of Marcus, Malcolm and Marley alongside flyers for a forthcoming event. The studio number has to be read out at regular intervals.

At five to twelve, it is time for us to go. The next DJ, Lady X, has arrived to play her set (soca only). Lady X is a black woman in her late forties/early fifties. She has a strong Bajan [Barbadian] accent. Fred unlocks the door for us and we make our way back to the car park downstairs. I turn on my radio. Lady X can be heard loud and clear.

(From field notes)

On the pirate stations the DJs pay subscription fees to the station owner. They are also required to read out or broadcast the paid-for advertisements. These

Figure 4.1 A wall at the pirate radio station: displaying the rules.

advertisements are not only for local events, but also for official government bodies such as the police's Crimestoppers initiative and the Department of Health anti-swine flu campaign.

Key businesses in the urban music economy

The four businesses foregrounded here are standalone but are interconnected in that all of these artist-entrepreneurs work across boundaries and have had a significant impact in the urban music sector. Previous tensions among performers have been resolved to move business and creativity forward and to ensure the widest possible audience for their music. Artists from N.A.S.T.Y crew and BBK have worked together – see Griminal – 'HAM' ft. JME as an example of this (griminal247365 2012).

Of the artist-entrepreneurs I interviewed, none had studied business or had formal qualifications or training in enterprise. Nevertheless, they had created networked identities as entrepreneurs and business owners and had adopted and domesticated technology early on to learn the rules of the game in this sector. According to data collected by the Federation of Small Businesses, the factors that underpin and influence the creation of new firms and business start-up include ability, need, opportunity, education and experience, as well as technology and innovation (Pickernell *et al.* 2013).

Accepted business theory indicates that venture capital, seed investment, mentors and bank loans are a requirement for successful start-up and growth. However, I have shown that for many in this sector, this is not the case. A small piece of equipment, such as a camera or having the opportunity to be coached or mentored by those already operating in the industry, can sometimes be enough of a catalyst to go beyond 'getting by' and start 'getting on' (Reynolds 2013). SBTV, an online broadcaster established initially as Smokey Barz TV in 2006 by 16-year-old Jamal Edwards, is a key example of a business that is 'getting on'. This channel now positions itself as an online youth broadcaster and has recently received capital investment (Smale 2013). At the time of writing it has achieved over 300 million views worldwide on YouTube. To mark the 100 millionth view, SBTV celebrated with a BBK (Boy Better Know) cipher[5] (smokeybarz 2012). BBK was initially a catchphrase for a grime crew from the Meridian Walk area of North London. It is now a registered trademark. It was established in 2005 by two brothers, Jamie and Junior Adenuga (who perform as JME and Skepta respectively), and its business output includes recording artists, a record label, a clothing line and a SIM card for a mobile phone network (Boy Better Know 2011). Carly Cussen is a music video director who started out at the age of sixteen.[6] At first, she produced urban music videos for young people who wanted to perform but had very limited means. Cussen has worked with almost every major grime artist, often on a shoestring budget. She has shot over 100 videos and has now graduated to creating videos for mainstream pop music acts such as Little Mix – *Hi How ya Doin'* (littlemixVEVO 2013) – and Olly Murs – *'Dear Darlin'* (OllyMursVEVO 2013). However, she continues to work with both signed and independent grime artists. Finally, N.A.S.T.Y crew started life as an east London grime crew in 2002. They have had a few subsequent incarnations, including N.A.S.T.Y UK and N.A.S.T.Y brothers. They consist of four brothers. Two are recording artists (Lil Narst and Griminal) and two perform as DJs (Marcus Nasty and Mak 10). As well as individual performance, their output includes a clothing line (Nasty by Nature), phone covers, a record label and an internet radio station (NastyCrew 2005; Nasty FM 2011; Nasty by Nature 2013).

These participants and my informants had had limited exposure to the social and cultural context of business. So, they learn to have a feel for this particular game by being mentored by an 'old hand' (still common in grime crews) or, perhaps, by observing someone who is making their mark in the sector. This particular social field, the urban music economy, allows my informants to fit into a business world. The business world that they operate in and are part of is, however, largely invisible, as it is obscured by a narrative of guns, gangs and postcode wars (Sherwin 2007; Curtis 2008; journeymanpictures 2008; Rose 2008; Panorama 2009). Perhaps this is because the wider business world has reproduced the concept of the entrepreneur in its own image, that is, the attributes and behaviour of the entrepreneur – risk-taking, innovation and so on, and is therefore not able to recognise entrepreneurs in the urban music economy. If they do, it is seen as an exception – such as Jamal Edwards – rather than the norm.

Creative enterprise: individual pursuits and collaborative practice

Participants in the urban music economy draw on the business practices and entrepreneurial spirit that are intrinsic components of both the Jamaican and UK sound systems (Witter 2004). For artist-entrepreneurs in this sector the context is, on the whole, one of low qualifications and poor employment prospects. Therefore enterprise – whether it takes the form of live performance, the staging of events, the sale of CDs, music downloads and other merchandise, DVDs, studio time, publicity or marketing materials – can afford opportunities, particularly where paid employment is scarce. Sometimes this may be the only way that young people from marginalised communities can have the kinds of jobs they desire in the creative economy.

Transformation in terms of entry into new identities is a real prospect for those that do participate, and this includes the former DJs, like Fred, who have now reinvented themselves as teachers and sell a neo-liberal concept of doing for self that is rooted in an imagined African-American construction of Africanness. Also, although the push for participation in this sector often comes from economic adversity, my informants also wanted to be financially autonomous, creative individuals, and they believed this was possible via self-employment and micro-entrepreneurship.

However, although it is evident that these entrepreneurs are 'buying in to neo-liberal capitalism' (Gilroy 2013, p. 34) in an individual attempt to overcome advanced marginality, this effort occurs at the same time as collective endeavour, and the 'bring in', or collaborative, activity is a key aspect of the urban music economy, nationally and internationally. There is also evidence of community activity as exemplified by UK grime artists JME and Skepta from BBK crew, who recently built a water pump in their father's village in Nigeria (JmeVerified account 2014). I contend that within the context of the urban music economy, economic enrichment is a collective enterprise as well as an individual one and it can offer a valid route to employment, albeit with the caveat that the endless demand from consumers for new product means that in many respects creative enterprise becomes something akin to a factory production line.

Conclusion

When I embarked on this project, I intended to map the creative practice in the 'underground' economy. However, at the initial phase, I soon discovered that there was a wide range of business types and models in place and that the participants carried out these activities, not underground, but on the ground and operated in much the same way as the formal sector. Microbusinesses, small businesses and self-employment in areas such as film directing, making music videos and the sale and distribution of clothing brands had been established in this sector. What was also evident was that, except in a few cases, these business owners applied their knowledge of their customer base in a pragmatic way, offering goods and services at low cost. Few mentioned that classroom or formal taught knowledge had any significance for the impetus for business start-up. These businesses emerged out of the individual passions of the artist-entrepreneurs and their desire to make money and become independent adults. Some of these ventures have grown to have a global presence, some have national and international reach, while others are almost entirely local. Nevertheless, business start-up, seen to be the lifeblood of the economy, is being generated by young people on shoestring budgets with access to very few resources.

At the start of my research project, I had not anticipated the global reach of grime, a type of music created in specific and particular urban areas in the UK. Over time, though, the genre mattered less than the opportunity it afforded to create an alternate persona: that of an entrepreneur and business owner. Indeed, seven of my informants played a pivotal role in setting up businesses that have a significant impact in the informal urban music economy.

Although an agreed definition for an entrepreneur or, indeed, for an enterprise culture is not in place, my research has shown that in the informal urban music economy, there is clear evidence of new ways of doing business. Examples include the innovative use of YouTube by SBTV or the SIM card created by Jamie Adenuga of BBK. The music industry may be the new 'road': it has replaced existing street tropes as a desired way of being for young people from impoverished areas. But, on the whole, my informants were not 'on road', and only two people referred to this (Ilan 2012). The activities of artists and entrepreneurs who have established and sustained businesses such as SBTV, BBK and NBN call for wider recognition as musicians and entrepreneurs. This entrepreneurial spirit and pride in achievements have emerged as new tropes for urban music artists.

Grime artists and other urban music practitioners are able to realise the means to consume as well as negotiate a dual repertoire of 'making it' and 'keeping it real', in other words creating a successful business while still maintaining credibility with the ends. But there is also a tension here between selling out and staying true to the game. Black vernacular cultures continue to have an ambivalent relationship with the corporate world (Gilroy 2004, p. 252). Wiley, the self-styled 'Godfather of Grime' and a founder of the grime scene, is an exemplar of this. He is signed to a major label – Warner – that brings him into contact with a wider audience.[7] Nonetheless, he still releases grime mixtapes – such as *Steps 1–20* – for free download, thereby operating simultaneously in both camps.

These artist-entrepreneurs have a tacit and detailed knowledge of their audience. Innovative use of technology has enabled them to turn their output into a commodity without needing an intermediary such as a record company. At the same time, audio and video production technology has become less expensive and therefore more accessible. This has created a juncture where micro-businesses could be created in the urban music industry, embodying what Ilan calls the 'respectable trope of the educated entrepreneur', meaning those who have stepped outside the boundaries of marginalisation (Ilan 2012). These business activities and networks, although founded in the UK, have a global reach.

Connections can be made, for example, between artists such as Skepta[8] from north London and internationally recognised artists such as P Diddy, Kanye West and Pharrell Williams. These business activities are not the efforts of mythical noble knights, but of people whose enterprise presents a different story to the usual.

Over a five-year period, I interviewed forty participants in the urban music economy, thirty-four of whom were artist-entrepreneurs. Most of the business activity conducted is represented here. These young people have responded to the challenges of the constant policy changes during their formal schooling years and shrinking economic opportunity to create business and enterprise. The learning and life strategies that they utilise include high levels of collaboration, which contests the predominant view that the lives of inner-city young people are defined by postcode silos. They also learn by doing, using and sharing available resources to produce and disseminate their creative output. Although I do not want to downplay the pressing challenges of urban life, such as that demonstrated by the civil disturbance in the UK in August 2011, I would argue that some convivial dimensions of diversity are in evidence here. Grime emerged from east London and it allows for an exploration of the disruption that occurs at the intersection of race and poverty.

Notes

1 Ofcom is the communications regulator. It regulates the TV and radio sectors, fixed-line telecoms and mobiles, plus the airwaves over which wireless devices operate. Ofcom operates under the Communications Act 2003.
2 A 'road' or 'hood' video is a music video created and recorded by unsigned artists.
3 So, 'accessible' broadcasting requires the completion of a video submission form as well as a non-exclusive license to broadcast. In addition, artists have to provide a vocal/instrumental mix of the track on CD. A biography, history, filmography, song lyrics and contact details are also required. Format is specified – videos must be submitted on BETA SP, DV CAM or MINI DV as PAL format. The broadcast quality is also tightly defined – 100% colour bars, audio should peak at – 6db and NO HIGHER, participants are required to double-check that vocals and pictures are in sync. Avoid flashing images. The video content requires the removal of all swear words and offensive, violent and racist language. There should be no reference to drugs or solvent abuse in a glamourised way. Product placement including websites, logos, is not permitted. Participants are also to ensure that all relevant permissions have been received.
4 The YouTube partnership programme is designed for regular video makers and offers a shared advertising revenue solution.
5 In this context, a 'cipher' is two or more rappers or MCs freestyling. It does not have to be a battle – they could be lyrically sparring or working off each other.
6 Carly Cussen filmed and directed Tinie Tempah's first video, 'Wifey', in 2006.
7 Wiley has been signed to major labels on a number of occasions, but is loathe to give up his artistic integrity to the mainstream.
8 In 2010, US hip-hop artist P Diddy invited Skepta to create a grime remix of his track *Hello – Good Morning*.

References

Albert, M.-N. and Couture, M.-M., 2013. The support to an entrepreneur: From autonomy to dependence. *SAGE Open*, 3(2). Available at: http://sgo.sagepub.com/content/3/2/2158244013492779.abstract.

Anderson, A., Drakopoulou Dodd, S. and Jack, S., 2009. Aggressors, winners, victims and outsiders. *International Small Business Journal*, 27(1), pp. 126–136.

Baumol, W.J., 1996. Entrepreneurship: Productive, unproductive, and destructive. *Journal of Business Venturing*, 11(1), pp. 3–22.

Boy Better Know, 2011. Boy Better Know SIM card – JME edition. *Boy Better Know*. Available at: www.boybetterknow.com/shop/Boy-Better-Know-Sim-Card-JME-Edition.html [accessed 15 April 2012].

Channel AKA, 2013. Channel AKA official. *Facebook*. Available at: www.facebook.com/CHANNELAKAOFFICIAL [accessed 2 February 2014].

Chell, E., 2007. Social enterprise and entrepreneurship: Towards a convergent theory of the entrepreneurial process. *International Small Business Journal*, 25(1), pp. 5–26.

Chen, M., 2007. *Rethinking the informal economy: Linkages with the formal economy and the formal regulatory environment*, United Nations Department of Economic and Social Affairs.

Collinson, J., 2006. Grime shouldn't pay. *Guardian*. Available at: www.guardian.co.uk/music/musicblog/2006/nov/08/grime [accessed 7 August 2010].

Cunningham, J.B. and Lischeron, J., 1991. Defining entrepreneurship. *Journal of Small Business Management*, 29(1).

Cunningham, S., 2012. Emergent innovation through the coevolution of informal and formal media economies. *Television & New Media*, 13(5), pp. 415–430.

Curtis, P., 2008. Youth crime: Greedy, rude adults 'fuelling teen violence'. *Guardian*. Available at: www.theguardian.com/education/2008/jul/11/schools.uk [accessed 20 October 2013].

Dennick, R., 2008. Theories of learning: Constructive experience. In *An Introduction to the Study of Education*, edited by David Matheson. London and New York: Routledge.

Drakopoulou Dodd, S. and Anderson, A.R., 2007. Mumpsimus and the mything of the individualistic entrepreneur. *International Small Business Journal*, 25(4), pp. 341–360.

Edwards, J., 2013. *Self belief – The vision: How to be a success on your own terms*, London, UK: Virgin Books.

Furlong, A. and Cartmel, F., 2007. *Young people and social change: New perspectives*, Maidenhead: McGraw-Hill/Open University Press.

Gerxhani, K., 2004. The informal sector in developed and less developed countries: A literature survey. *Public Choice*, 120(3), pp. 267–300.

Gilroy, P., 1993. *Small acts: Thoughts on the politics of black cultures*, London, UK: Serpents Tail.

Gilroy, P., 2004. *Between camps: Nations, cultures and the allure of race*, London: Routledge.

Gilroy, P., 2013. "…We got to get over before we go under…" fragments for a history of black vernacular neoliberalism. *New Formations*, (80/81).

Grabiner, A.S., 2000. *The informal economy: A report*, London, UK: HM Treasury.

griminal247365, 2012. *Griminal ft. JME – HAM*. Available at: www.youtube.com/watch?v=0ANe9nyFTZk&feature=youtube_gdata_player [accessed 20 June 2012].

Gunter, A., 2010. *Growing up bad? Black youth, road culture and badness in an east London neighbourhood*, London, UK: Tufnell Press.

Heale, J., 2008. *One blood: Inside Britain's new street gangs*, London, UK: Simon & Schuster.

Hill Collins, P., 2006. New commodities, new consumers. Selling blackness in a global marketplace. *Ethnicities*, 6(3), pp. 297–317.

Ilan, J., 2012. 'The industry's the new road': Crime, commodification and street cultural tropes in UK urban music. *Crime, Media, Culture*, 8(1), pp. 39–55.

Imas, J.M., Wilson, N. and Weston, A., 2012. Barefoot entrepreneurs. *Organization*, 19(5), pp. 563–585.

JmeVerified account, 2014. RT @Skepta: Fresh water pump we had made for everybody in my Dad's village in Nigeria finally finished. Emotional … http://instagram.com/p/quVFkjTDkw/. *@JmeBBK*. Available at: https://twitter.com/JmeBBK/status/49136014 2521532416 [accessed 26 November 2014].

Johansson, A.W., 2004. Narrating the entrepreneur. *International Small Business Journal*, 22(3), pp. 273–293.

journeymanpictures, 2008. *London Gangs – UK*. Available at: www.youtube.com/watch?v=4YH0LUt8R2k&feature=youtube_gdata_player [accessed 16 September 2010].

Keyes, C.L., 2004. *Rap music and street consciousness*, Champaign, IL: University of Illinois Press.

Leadbeater, C., 2009. *We-Think: Mass innovation, not mass production*, 2nd edn, London, UK: Profile Books.

littlemixVEVO, 2013. *Little Mix – How Ya Doin'? ft. Missy Elliott*. Available at: www.youtube.com/watch?v=hT_HWIIKbG8&feature=youtube_gdata_player [accessed 13 July 2013].

Llanes, M. and Barbour, A., 2007. Self-employed and micro-entrepreneurs: Informal trading and the journey towards formalisation. London: Community Links.

Losby, J.L., Else, J.F., Kingslow, M.E., Edgcomb, E.L, Malm, E.T. and Kao, V., 2002. Informal economy literature review. Institute for Social and Economic Development (ISED) and Microenterprise Fund for Innovation, Effectiveness, Learning, and Dissemination (FIELD).

Low, M.B. and MacMillan, I.C., 1988. Entrepreneurship: Past research and future challenges. *Journal of Management*, 14(2), pp. 139–161.

Macdonald, R., Shildrick, T. and Furlong, A., 2013. In search of 'intergenerational cultures of worklessness': Hunting the yeti and shooting zombies. *Critical Social Policy*. Available at: http://csp.sagepub.com/content/early/2013/09/26/0261018313501825.abstract.

Muir, H., 2006. Rapper who killed producer for 'disrespect' gets 30 years. *Guardian*. Available at: www.guardian.co.uk/uk/2006/nov/03/ukguns.musicnews [accessed 7 August 2010].

Murray, S. and Gayle, V., 2012. *Youth transitions*, University of Stirling.

Nasty by Nature, 2013. #NBNOS. *Nasty by Nature Online Store*. Available at: www.nastybynature.co.uk/store/ [accessed 13 July 2013].

NastyCrew, 2005. N.A.S.T.Y | Free Music, Tour Dates, Photos, Videos. Available at: www.myspace.com/nastycrew2007 [accessed 24 August 2011].

Nasty FM, 2011. Home | Nasty.fm – Streaming Grime, Dubstep and more Live 24/7. *Nasty FM*. Available at: www.nasty.fm [accessed 1 March 2011].

Ofcom, 2013. *The Office of Communications Annual Report and Accounts*, London: The Stationery Office.

OllyMursVEVO, 2013. *Olly Murs – Dear Darlin'*. Available at: www.youtube.com/watch?v=m20BTdy9FGI&feature=youtube_gdata_player [accessed 13 July 2013].

Panorama, 2009. 'We will come for you', gangs warned. *BBC*. Available at: http://news.bbc.co.uk/panorama/hi/front_page/newsid_8366000/8366280.stm [accessed 1 December 2010].

Pickernell, D., Senyard, J., Jones, P., Packham, G. and Ramsey, E 2013. New and young firms: Entrepreneurship policy and the role of government – evidence from the Federation of Small Businesses survey. *Journal of Small Business and Enterprise Development*, 20(2), pp. 358–382.

Redhead, S., Wynne, D. and O'Connor, J., eds., 1998. *Clubcultures Reader: Readings in Popular Cultural Studies*, Oxford, UK and Malden, MA: Wiley-Blackwell.

Reynolds, T., 2013. 'Them and us': 'Black neighbourhoods' as a social capital resource among black youths living in inner-city London. *Urban Studies*, 50(3), pp. 484–498.

Rose, A., 2008. Teenage knife and gun fatalities hit an all-time high. *Guardian*. Available at: www.guardian.co.uk/world/2008/dec/28/knife-crime-deaths-eyewitness [accessed 9 July 2012].

Schneider, F., 2004. Size and measurement of the informal economy in 110 countries. Unpublished conference paper presented at a workshop of the Australian National Tax Centre, Australian National University, Canberra, Australia, 17 July 2002.

Schoof, U., 2006. *Stimulating youth entrepreneurship: Barriers and incentives to enterprise start-ups by young people*, Geneva: International Labour Office.

Schumpeter, J.A., 1994. *Capitalism, socialism and democracy*, Hove, UK: Psychology Press.

Sherwin, A., 2007. Pirate radio DJs risk prosecution to fight gun and knife crime. *Times Online*. Available at: www.timesonline.co.uk/tol/news/uk/article2288801.ece [accessed 24 August 2011].

Smale, W., 2013. Amateur film-maker turned media boss. *BBC*. Available at: www.bbc.co.uk/news/business-24801980 [accessed 4 January 2014].

smokeybarz, 2012. *Boy Better Know | 100M YouTube views – [CYPHER]: SBTV*. Available at: www.youtube.com/watch?v=Ei09chGK2EM&feature=youtube_gdata_player [accessed 13 July 2013].

Stevenson, H.H. and Jarillo, J.C., 1990. A paradigm of entrepreneurship: Entrepreneurial management. *Strategic Management Journal 11*, pp. 17–27.

Stickler, A., 2008. Guns and knives on the streets. *BBC*. Available at: http://news.bbc.co.uk/today/hi/today/newsid_7773000/7773718.stm [accessed 20 October 2013].

Tanzi, V., 1999. Uses and abuses of estimates of the underground economy. *The Economic Journal*, 109(456), pp. 338–347.

Tomlinson, S., 2005. *Education in a post-welfare society*, 2nd edn, Maidenhead, UK: Open University Press.

Venkatesh, S., 2002. Doin' the hustle. *Ethnography*, 3(1), pp. 91–111.

White, J., 2014. (In)visible entrepreneurs: Creative enterprise in the urban music economy. In K. Rene, ed., *Beyond frames: Dynamics between the creative industries, knowledge institutions and the urban context*, pp. 88–95.

Williams, C.C., 2006. *The hidden enterprise culture: Entrepreneurship in the underground economy*, Cheltenham, UK and Northampton, MA: Edward Elgar Publishing.

Witter, M., 2004. *Music and the Jamaican economy*, Prepared for UNCTAD/WIPO.

Wolfson, S., 2013. Giggs: Prison, police harassment, cancelled tours: When will it stop? *Guardian*. Available at: www.theguardian.com/music/2013/oct/05/giggs-when-will-it-stop [accessed 10 November 2013].

Part III
Crossing borders

5 Enterprise abroad

A case study from Ayia Napa

I got a few events lined up, plus you get more of a name for yourself if you merk[1] out of Ayia Napa. You can't be a part of a scene and not make yourself visible, you know coming out here to Napa, it's all about getting to know everyone and making music.

(Tyrone, 18 – MC – interviewed in 2009)

Introduction

Grime is an oral narrative that exhorts the perspectives of 'the ends'. Grime, a cultural form that navigates and articulates experiences of curtailment, bordering and exclusion in inner-city east London, had an established footprint in the UK and Europe. By the summer of 2009, UK funky had emerged as a new genre, and many luminaries of the grime scene became actively involved. For young people planning holidays, a variety of factors come into play, but the desire to pursue musical tastes abroad is a key motivation. For a number of years, tour operators have put together packages to attract this audience. Social media and radio stations, both pirate and licensed, also promote the hype that accompanies and encourages participation in the international party arena.

Far from being a highly localised, niche creative practice, the act of creating grime music propels its practitioners into the world and away from 'the ends'. During the interviews, and while I was exploring the artistic output of the grime scene online and on radio, it became apparent to me that although the respondents were grounded in east London through residence or performance or both, their reach and influence extended far beyond this locale. In the UK I found evidence grime had an audience and a steady demand for live performance outside of London. In Swindon and Bristol, for example, the Sidewinder events provided a platform for MCs and DJs (Sidewinder 2006, 2007),[2] and Eskimo Dance occasions took luminaries of the grime scene to Watford and beyond (NuthingSorted.com 2006). In this chapter, I use the Ayia Napa experience as a case study to explore how urban music has further enabled markets and primary and secondary business activities to be created and developed in a national and global context. A key location for the participants in the informal urban music economy was the summer season in the resort of Ayia Napa in southern Cyprus.

Charting the journey from garage to funky house[3]

The current musical scene in Ayia Napa is the latest stopping-off point on a ten-year journey that takes us from garage to grime and from grime to UK funky, underpinned by, and sonically connected to, dancehall, bashment and bassline. This musical scene is a cultural space that contains a wide range of coexisting musical practices, each impacting and influencing the other (Will Straw in Redhead *et al.* 1998). The genres shift and change, but the enterprising activity remains. These urban music genres are rooted in and have developed out of black diaspora music culture. The grime scene is a cornerstone of the current informal music economy. It is a particularly London-based urban creative expression. Grime draws its influences from the sound systems of Jamaica, filtered through the last few decades of hip-hop, drum and bass and two-step garage. In the early years of the twenty-first century, it rose from the gritty terrain of inner-city east London. As a music genre, grime has its origins in the hybridity of reggae, North American R n B and hip-hop, which itself grew out of the black Atlantic exchange between North American and Caribbean musical expression. This urban art form is an 'invented musical expression' (Gilroy 1993, p. 76) that draws on the cultural, political and economic history of having parents and grandparents from elsewhere and of staking a claim to the lived experience of a specific and particular place, in this case urban east London.

Now, there is a specific and particular audience from the United Kingdom who come to participate in a musical scene that has been temporarily transplanted from the urban environment of inner-city London to the third largest island in the Mediterranean – Cyprus. For approximately three months every summer, the resort of Ayia Napa is transformed from a sleepy village into a thriving holiday resort. Tourism is a key part of the Cypriot economy, and every year roughly two million holidaymakers arrive from all over Europe. The majority of those that come – 56 per cent – are British (Ministry of Finance 2010). Britain shares a long colonial past with Cyprus and still has two Sovereign Base Areas (SBAs) on the island (The British Army 2013). In the London Borough of Newham in east London there is an area called Cyprus that is so named to commemorate the UK taking over government of the island from the Ottoman Empire in 1878. Over the last ten years, the urban music genres detailed above have established themselves in this location, creating a vital market for events, merchandise and performance.

'What happens in Ayia Napa is broadcast on YouTube…'

I knew from my initial research that the urban music community is constantly recording and being recorded (on cameras, camcorders and mobile phones); filming is a standard and quotidian activity. Technology is used by both participants and practitioners to create a significant and highly visible public presence. Channel AKA, YouTube, Facebook and MySpace were used extensively to promote creative output, goods, services and experiences both in the UK and throughout Europe. During the interviews, it also became apparent that there was one particular DJ, Victor, who many of the respondents had collaborated with or aspired to work with. Starting out as one of the founder members of an east London grime collective, it also emerged that he was a key player in the Ayia Napa scene. I had listened to Victor's regular show on pirate radio and been a participant at one of his London events. Now, the search for him in Ayia Napa became the baseline for my field research in this location.

The marketing campaign in the UK for the musical scene in Ayia Napa begins several months before with pre-parties, events and reunions happening all over the UK. So, in August 2009, armed with an HD film camera and a friend, I decided to record the journey from east London to southern Cyprus, to make and experience the movement that the artists had made and to talk to people at different stages of the journey. Before I left, I interviewed Edward and Andrew again because both of them had recently returned from performing in the clubs there. From my initial research, it seemed that this is very much a raucous party resort. It was also evident from existing footage that there are distinct segments to 'the vibe', the beach, the club and the after-party, and my plan was to observe the activities and speak to people in each setting (ASITISTV 2006; bushbashents 2008; NSCProductions 2009).

At the airport(s): Gatwick and Larnaca

The cost of the journey is a factor, as Cyprus is relatively expensive compared to other Mediterranean destinations, such as Spain, that are popular with UK travellers. Holidays in this resort are at a premium, and therefore all of the experience counts and needs to be savoured. The holidaymakers I spoke to had come from all parts of the UK and they had gone to Ayia Napa for 'the vibe'.[4] And it is 'the vibe' as a concept constructed by these urban artists that is a key organising principle of the music scene and economy in Ayia Napa. 'The vibe' is centred on DJs, MCs and various events promoted and coordinated either by the artists themselves or by specific promoters. Getting on the plane at Gatwick, I spoke to three young women (two from Birmingham and one from Chiswick in west London) who were going to Ayia Napa for the first time. Once I landed I also had a brief conversation with two girls from Tewkesbury. All of these young women were going to Ayia Napa because of the music: they wanted to see JME and Skepta and listen to grime and UK funky. For Tom, a dubstep event promoter from New Cross in south London, it was the whole package: 'music, cheap drinks, the whole party vibe'.

I had planned to take a taxi from Larnaca airport but realised that most of the holidaymakers were on a package, which included a shuttle transfer from the airport to their hotels. When I disembarked from the plane, I interviewed Tom, the event promoter from New Cross, before being asked by the Cypriot police to turn the camera off. The holiday rep agreed that we could get on the bus, and I almost got to film a female MC 'freestyling',[5] but again we were told to shut the camera down. For the participants, the camera offered an opportunity for their performance to be recorded and broadcast. However, for the police and the holiday company, the camera represented a threat either to security or to company reputation.

At the hotel

I had chosen this particular hotel as it appeared to be a popular destination for the young tourists from the UK. I arrive in the early hours of the morning. While a small group of us waits to check in, a young man staggers into the lobby, clearly very intoxicated. He asks each of us in turn if we know which hotel he is staying in. After a few minutes, his friend comes in and takes him away. While I wait to check in, I notice a pool of vomit by the reception desk, next to the public phone. The receptionist, who becomes aware of it at the same time that I do, leaves her desk, places a stool in front of the now congealing puddle and then returns to her desk and carries on with her work. I wonder how I am going to survive this experience.

In the morning, I sit on the balcony and as my room is on the ground floor, I watch people going to and from the pool. It is fairly quiet as most people do not wake up until early afternoon. So I go for a walk and identify the main locations (and the car hire, buggy hire and 'ped hire spots) on the streets that constitute 'the strip'. By late afternoon, more people surface and make their way towards the pool. Initially, I speak to three young men of Greek Cypriot descent who have travelled from Palmers Green. They tell me that they stay for six weeks every year as they have family there. I explain that I am looking for Victor. There is an immediate recognition: 'I saw him two days ago, when I was in the barber's getting my hair cut' (from field notes).

I speak briefly to other people at the poolside to find out what has brought them to the resort. The majority are under the age of 30 and have come for 'the vibe'. It is the music and the atmosphere it creates that is the main draw for these holidaymakers. While I am talking to a group of ten girls from the West Midlands, Xavier, a secondary school teacher from south London, introduces himself to me. Xavier has been in the resort for several weeks. This week he is promoting his event, 'Funkie Junkie', at Drench. Just before we sit down to talk, Xavier and his colleague have been distributing promotional flyers around the pool. All of the billed artists are from the UK, and I ask Xavier where I might find Victor, who I notice is the headline act on the flyer. He suggests Nissi Beach, where most of the artists are during the day; otherwise, later on, Drench. Xavier is relatively new to the events market in Ayia Napa, but he has experience as a promoter in London. He is relying on the billed artists to be a big enough draw to fill the club. When I ask him what motivates him to do this, he says: 'well, it's basic maths: six hundred people per venue, times ten pounds, equals six thousand pounds'. During our talk, Xavier tells me that he is the 'boss of the "Funkie Junkie" team'. I say something I think is non-committal and unassuming in return, but he starts to bristle. He asks me why I look surprised. I am not aware that I have expressed such a reaction, but then I realise that he has an audience to play to (the young women from the Midlands) and, not wanting to offend him, I explain that he looks young to be a boss. He seems satisfied with this and, ego intact, proffers me smile and a flyer and suggests I come to the club later.

On the beach

Nissi Beach hosts the daytime activities for many of the holidaymakers. So we hire a buggy and drive for a very bumpy ten minutes to the beach. Today, a north London crew, Animo, provides the beach entertainment. Although each of the three members of this crew are just thirty years old, they have been performers, artists, MCs and DJs for more than fifteen years. Starting out performing in house parties and clubs, Animo now command a business that draws its audience from all over the UK and Europe. When I look around the beach, very few artists are wearing or displaying a brand that is not theirs, and Animo are no exception: they and their workers wear T-shirts that promote their regular Thursday night event at Sugar. These young men are at the top of their game, selling their own branded merchandise, pre-booked by club owners throughout the summer season, and also promoting their own weekly events. The presence of a good quality HD camera meant that people were more willing to speak to me. For example, when seeking permission for the first interview on Nissi Beach, Kevin, an MC and event promoter with Animo, says: 'If it had just been any youth wanting me to jump into one of their road videos, I would have said no, but I can see you're serious' (from field notes).

Throughout the interview, Kevin is polite, charming and articulate. He is clearly used to telling his story and narrates his personal history with ease. His crew have worked through and with a variety of urban music genres. I have also seen them provide cameo roles in recent films with an urban theme. At the end of our interview, Kevin excuses himself and asks me to stay around for the entertainment in about fifteen minutes time. Once the performance starts however, Kevin is transformed. While another member of the Animo crew plays the tracks, Kevin hosts a variety of ever more spirited and entertaining beach games for the tourists on the beach.

Haircuts and curry goat: finding a gap in the market

After this first interview with Kevin on Nissi Beach, respondents were, on the whole, self-selecting. Kevin is relatively well known in the urban music economy, so once people had seen him talking to me, they asked to be interviewed as well. Some respondents also wanted to promote themselves and their business activities. Lionel was one of them.

Lionel was in Ayia Napa promoting his latest business venture and asked if he could be interviewed. Lionel had come to the resort the previous year as a holidaymaker. He had realised after a couple of weeks that his hair was starting to look untidy – and not 'crisp' how he liked it. So, after discussion with his business partners, he had returned this year and set up a barbershop 'specialising in fades and shape ups'. Lionel gave me his business card and a leaflet and told me that his barbershop was 'around the corner' from the Caribbean restaurant.

For Lionel, enterprise and being an entrepreneur meant spotting a gap in the market and acting on it. In response to my question about whether he had a background in the music industry, he replied: 'No, I'm just an entrepreneur. I'm someone that sees an opportunity and I go for it. I've also got a T-shirt company back home called "My Hood" just launching'. During his interview, Lionel also announced the details for his website. He was also keen to point out the breadth of his client base:

> So here we are, yeah *Fades and Shades* barbershop, official barber shop of Ayia Napa and we got all of the top DJs coming through now: Martin Larner, Marcus Nasty, DJ EJ from up North. We got a lot of people coming, and the locals as well; we don't just cut black peoples hair, we got white, Cypriot.
>
> (Lionel, 30 – barber)

After I had finished talking to Lionel. I bought a drink and sat down in the shade. Oliver had positioned himself so he was seated on the wall behind me. He made sure that I knew he had something to say, by conducting a detailed and fairly loud phone conversation. He made sure that all those around him knew that he was checking the progress of the distribution of his product. Once he had finished with his phone call, I introduced myself, explained what I was doing in the resort and asked him if he would mind talking to me on camera. Oliver, an MC and DJ with many years experience, had no doubts about his reasons for being here, to promote himself and his products and services:

> Yeah, I'm from that crew … originally. I got a tune out at the moment called 'Funky Rush'. Yeah, I'm just in Ayia Napa working. I'm going out to the northern part of the island and then I'm coming back here on Monday. Yeah, I'm promoting my tune 'Funky Rush', and I've got a drink coming out called 'Funky Rush' – an energy drink.
>
> (Oliver, 30 – MC/producer)

Oliver felt his reputation was such that he did not really need the Ayia Napa exposure to heighten his visibility or his credibility: 'to be honest, I'm not one of them guys who need Ayia Napa to make money … but it is vital to be seen … I'll be real with you, this island is not much of a business' (Oliver, 30 – MC/ producer).

A few weeks later, back in London, I found the website and the Facebook page for 'Funky Rush' – both the track and the energy drink. Oliver saw himself as an old hand because of his past experience as a member of a relatively successful grime crew.[6] He had been coming to Ayia Napa for many years and in various guises, and while we talked, he pointed out someone who, in his opinion, was a rising star – a young man called Richard. This young man was 18 and had not left the UK before. He told me that what had brought him here from an estate of poor repute in Harlesden (in north-west London) was the chance to promote himself to a relevant audience and become more recognised. As an unsigned artist his video had received 800,000 views on YouTube. Richard slipped into his performance persona and gave an impromptu rendition of his current track to a gathering audience. Oliver, who was still sitting on the wall, provided the ad-lib input[7] for the act. One of Richard's companions did not want to be seen in the video, so he covered his face and moved out of shot. Once Richard had finished, he said that in his opinion, Ayia Napa 'wasn't all that, just a hype ting with the same hood people'. He disappeared into the crowd, so I did not get an opportunity to explore this further with him.

I failed to find Victor on Nissi Beach. Instead, I met one of his MCs, Quentin, who told me that Victor was playing at a pool party in one of the hotels. Quentin, like the others, wanted to be interviewed, but I had run out of film. Quentin told me that he and Victor would be at Drench later on, so I agreed to interview him there.

At the club

At about midnight, we make our way to Drench, where Victor is the headline act. To get to the square where the clubs are, I have to walk down 'the strip', which because of the camera involves negotiating brief interviews at roughly two-minute intervals. What should be a fifteen-minute journey takes forty-five minutes. Nevertheless, while walking I meet people who have come from all over the UK, some of whom are working – for example Candy, a young woman from Sheffield, is doing PR for Animo, distributing flyers for tomorrow night's event. Others are in full party mode, carousing in the street. Outside Drench we film some of them for about ten minutes to capture the feel of the scene. It is very, very loud and bustling with people.

In the bar adjacent to Drench, three dancers dressed in skimpy bikinis hang loosely from poles. I gradually become more accustomed to the noise. And then I spot Victor emerging from the crowd. His headphones are around his neck and he is carrying a small CD case. I introduce myself. He laughs and says that he has already heard that there is a film crew looking for him. I give him a brief outline of what I am doing and then ask him whether I can interview him on camera inside the club. He asks me to hold on and then goes over to speak to the club owner: 'This is my film crew, is it alright for them to come?' The club owner agrees. Victor beckons us inside. The club has not opened yet, so we select and set up in a good location, in the bar area at the back.

The doors open at 1:00 a.m., and the club is soon at full capacity – with approximately 600 people and the entrance fee ten euros, Xavier's calculations are correct give or take the euro exchange rate. If it was loud outside, the volume is even greater in the club, and even though we have positioned ourselves at the back of the club, it is still a very noisy space. Once the camera is set up most respondents put themselves forward for interview, except William, who is a little hesitant, so Victor brings him over and makes the introduction. I speak to all except one of the artists who are performing. Some of them have taken time off work and have fit this particular enterprising activity around their everyday – that is formal, regulated and taxed identities of, for example, the electrician or the secondary school teacher; others are operating entirely off the books, but one respondent, who is also playing tonight, has a regular show on a national radio station (he started out as a member of a UK sound system, playing a variety of urban music some fifteen years ago). Another, William, the 19-year-old music producer from Reading, had left the UK for the first time to come to Ayia Napa. When I speak to him he has been in Cyprus for a week and is planning to stay for one more, depending on the work offers he receives. Michael has taken two weeks off work in Wolverhampton to come to Ayia Napa to promote the bassline sound. He describes his journey from being an MC to becoming a DJ playing old-school garage, grime, funky and now bassline:

> Well, basically, I'm trying to promote the sound, tryng to push the whole bassline sound in Ayia Napa, because knowing that Ayia Napa is where everybody comes along, from North, South, East, West, different countries, an' that, so basically I just took the chance to try and push myself ... so when they go back they think, yeah, that bassline sound, that's DJ Michael.
>
> (Michael, 33 – DJ)

Quentin, who I had met on the beach earlier that day, is the host tonight for Victor's set. As an MC/host his job is to 'pick up the vibe that the DJ is trying to create'. Quentin has also taken time off work to be here. An older hand in this setting is Peter. He has come for the weekend only because he now has a show on a national radio station for five nights a week. Peter has learned his craft through the sound system and pirate radio route. He has also played a variety of genres throughout the years, including garage and dancehall.

Finally, I interview Victor, the DJ in the informal music economy who I have been trying to interview for two years. Victor describes himself as a DJ and talent scout. Like Kevin, the MC from Animo crew who I met earlier that day on Nissi Beach, he is polished and at ease in front of the camera. In response to my question about 'what next', he laughs and says: 'Hopefully, some TV presenting'. He outlines how he started out in an east London grime crew some ten years before and identifies some of the artists from that crew, which had achieved mainstream success. Since then, Victor explains, DJ'ing has taken him to locations around the UK and abroad. His creative practice has enabled him to establish fan bases in countries he had not yet been to. He also describes how, four years before, he had anticipated a shift in the urban music scene, and outlines the activities he undertook to ensure that a market was created for this new musical style:

> And I introduced it [UK funky] to all the DJs: it's pointless me being the top guy in a small scene; I need to be the top guy in a big scene. The only way

to make the scene grow is to get everyone involved and that's what I'm trying to do right now. All the producers from A... to D... to K..., they'll tell you that I've marketed them myself for nothing, no personal gain, but for the scene to grow, do know what I mean, and now this is what it is, if you go anywhere along this strip in Ayia Napa you'll hear funky.

(Victor, 33 – DJ)

Victor is clearly proud of his achievements and of how he has used his influence to create a growing market, and therefore employment for many, in this emerging music genre. As a participant enjoying music and the whole club scene, I have not really taken too much notice of what the DJ or the sound system do. As a participant, I just know if they are skilled at their task or not. The best ones can stir you up or mellow you out; they take you on a journey and let you know when to head for the bar, when to strut your stuff on the dance floor and when to head home. However, as a participant observer, I become increasingly aware of the multiplicity of skills that are involved in working in this confined space, in judging the mood to select and play the right track, in coordinating with the actions of the MC or host, and in communicating what is coming next, often non-verbally. When I observe Victor perform at his Drench set, I watch as he indicates to his MCs, sometimes with just a look or a nod of the head, what track he is going to play next. At the same time, there is an insistent and compelling intensity to the performance that makes it impossible not to join in.

After the after-party

Once the clubs close, the after-party is another key business activity. At 7:00 a.m., as the refuse collectors clear up the debris from the night before, I meet Neville, an event promoter who started his career as an MC and who has been coming to Ayia Napa for ten years. Neville stays on location for the whole season – six to eight weeks – promoting his weekly after-party event at another popular club, Ravine. It has an entrance fee of ten euro, and customers are given a free T-shirt with every ticket.

I end my visit to the island with a trip to the Caribbean restaurant that Lionel has told me about a few days before and enjoy the national Jamaican dish – ackee and saltfish – washed down with a traditional fruit punch. The restaurant has a Jamaican chef – who now lives in Wales for the rest of the year. I talk with the owners and ask them what brings them to Ayia Napa. They confirm that they come because they are aware that there is a more substantial market for their services and products during the summer season in this resort than if they stayed in Barry Island in Wales.

My Ayia Napa case study offers some evidence that the urban music economy, far from being hyperlocal, actually conducts its business over a wide geographical reach, both in the UK and globally. There perhaps was a time when it was possible to speak of a 'creative underground', as Bradley suggests:

A blues dance, late at night, in the heart of the black neighbourhood, publicised by word of mouth, or flyers in record shops or other blues, were about
as underground as you were going to get in mainland Britain in 1970.

(Bradley 2000, p. 378)

Now, however, almost all urban music events happen in highly regulated venues
with a plethora of related laws and regulations, for example licensing and health
and safety laws. The shebeen, blues dance and nomadic rave event, once subjected to the 'disciplinary procedures which organise social space' have been
legislated out of existence (Stanley-Niaah 2004). Nevertheless, it is possible that
these disciplinary procedures, combined with the discourse regarding urban creative expression, have enabled a countermovement – a music scene in which
urban youth and young black men in particular can create a new persona as
perhaps an artist or an entrepreneur. This in turn allows entry into a different
assemblage – that of the economic marketplace. This black Atlantic trajectory
takes us to a space twenty-five miles from Africa, where a marketplace has been
created through the entrepreneurial activities of young men of Caribbean descent
travelling from predominantly urban environments in the UK. The black Atlantic
in this context is a cultural construction that goes beyond the geographical and
physical boundaries of Africa, the Caribbean and the United States. When
Animo perform on Nissi Beach in Ayia Napa, creating 'the vibe' by using all
styles of urban music (and including Jamaican bashment), we experience what
Soja calls that 'triple dialogue of space, time and social being' as young people
from the UK participate in the urban music economy both as producers and consumers (Hubbard *et al.* 2004, p. 270).

Conclusion

The market for 'the vibe' in Ayia Napa is evidence of how the informal sector
exists in a symbiotic relationship with the formal economy. Event promoters do
not distinguish between 'underground' DJs and MCs and 'legal' DJs; their
concern is to attract a paying audience.

One of my respondents in the UK was George, a music producer who operated primarily in the informal economy. While George was talking about trying
to get his tracks played on the radio, he said: 'If you like there's an executive
board with Hotsteppa, Marcus Nasty and Supa D at the top'. Getting your tunes
played by these DJs guarantees exposure and therefore success becomes more
likely, the point being that Hotsteppa is on a legal radio station and Supa D and
Marcus Nasty are on pirate stations, yet all three have the same value in terms of
influence and impact in this market. I carried out my field research in 2009.
Since then Rinse FM has become legal. After fourteen years as a pirate station, it
now has a licence to broadcast from Ofcom.

Rather than shrinking, the informal sector adapts and appears in novel
formats. In the urban music economy, the customer and the procurer of services
make little distinction between those that are provided by participants in the

Figure 5.1 A banner outside a popular club on 'the strip' in Ayia Napa featuring DJs from the formal and informal urban music economy.

formal or informal sector. Often, the activities are so embedded there is little to separate them; for example, artists and entrepreneurs in the informal economy use officially registered social networking sites and websites to advertise their services and products. At the same time, official agencies such as the Metropolitan Police and the Department of Health regularly run advertising campaigns on pirate radio. These radio stations operate from unlicensed venues under the watchful eye of regulatory bodies like Ofcom. Yet the prevailing discourse regarding the urban music economy still assumes that it is never part of the mainstream and that it operates in some distant and unreachable place.

Enterprise in the UK and in Ayia Napa takes the form of events, performance and merchandise, such as CDs/mixtapes and clothing. At the core are MCs, DJs, music producers, vocalists, beat makers and event promoters. My informants had travelled from their inner-city areas to promote themselves and their creative practice in a setting that was a far cry from their urban environments.

Generally, enterprise culture is seen to take place in a clean and sanitised way. This might be a key reason why literature and research into enterprise have not, on the whole, included the informal economy. The informal economy is in fact an enduring sector in developed countries, but little research has been carried out to show how the underground and informal spheres are linked. My field research in Ayia Napa provides evidence of the borderless flow of this creative expression and makes it clear that these sectors (formal and informal) do not operate side by side or on the ground/underground, but are inextricably linked, as each sector requires the other.

Notes

1 To 'merk' means to kill the opposition lyrically.
2 MCs and DJs from London who performed at these events include, in Swindon, Cameo, Mac 10, Marcus Nasty, Logan Sama, Heartless Crew, Hyper Fen, Stormin, Ghetto, Scorcher, Ultra, Cheeky, Bearman, Viper, Wiley, Skepta, Donaeo, and JME; and, in Bristol, Cameo, Snakeyman, Semtex, Ras Kwame, Broke 'n' English, Doctor, L.Man, Hypa Fenn & Marcie Phonix, Wiley, JME, Skepta and Faith SFX.
3 Garage and funky house are urban music genres, as are grime, dancehall, bashment and bassline. All are rooted in and have developed out of black diaspora music culture.
4 'The vibe' is a sensation, a collection of moments and feelings that shapes an individual's personal experience of the event. It includes, in this context, a dynamic relationship between the audience and the performers.
5 'Freestyling' is an impromptu or unplanned performance.
6 Since this interview, his performance on one track has been featured in the soundtrack of a Hollywood film.
7 An 'ad-lib' in this context means contributing additional words or sounds to emphasise words and phrases.

References

ASITISTV, 2006. *Ayia Napa 2002*. Available at: www.youtube.com/watch?v=wae7iPGR N3Y&feature=youtube_gdata_player [accessed 24 December 2010].

Bradley, L., 2000. *Bass culture: When reggae was king*, London, UK: Viking.

bushbashents, 2008. *Female skanker of Ayia Napa 08: The beach party, Best of Part 1*. Available at: www.youtube.com/watch?v=Q_Uxom2ckSU&feature=youtube_gdata_ player [accessed 5 February 2011].

Gilroy, P., 1993. *Small acts: Thoughts on the politics of black cultures*, London, UK and New York: Serpents Tail.

Hubbard, P., Kitchin, R. and Valentine, G., 2004. *Key thinkers on space and place*, London, California, New Delhi and Singapore: Sage Publications.

Ministry of Finance, 2010. *Statistical Service*. Available at: www.mof.gov.cy/mof/cystat/ statistics.nsf/services_71main_en/services_71main_en?OpenForm&sub=1&sel=2 [accessed 24 June 2016].

NSCProductions, 2009. *The official Ayia Napa send off, Saturday 13th June 09, Club Demand, Coventry*. Available at: www.youtube.com/watch?v=jPEywOwHfLM&featur e=youtube_gdata_player [accessed 5 February 2011].

NuthingSorted.com, 2006. The eskimo dance presents … the UK link up at Area (Watford), 16 February 2006, event listing. Available at: www.nuthingsorted.com/ index.php?sID=12237633067259 [accessed 16 November 2013].

Redhead, S., Wynne, D. and O'Connor, J., eds, 1998. *Clubcultures reader: Readings in popular cultural studies*, Oxford, UK and Malden, MA: Wiley-Blackwell.

Sidewinder, 2006. Sidewinder, Tommorow Night! Brunel Rooms, Swindon!! ITS GRIII-IME. Available at: www.hijackbristol.co.uk/board/the-forum/sidewinder-tommorow-night!-brunel-rooms-swindon!!-its-griiiime/?wap2 [accessed 16 November 2013].

Sidewinder, 2007. Love music hate racism, Sidewinder – Bristol Carling Academy. Available at: http://lovemusichateracism.com/2007/05/sidewinder-bristol-carling-academy [accessed 16 November 2013].

Stanley-Niaah, S., 2004. Kingston's dancehall: A story of space and celebration. *Space and Culture*, 7(1), pp. 102–118.

The British Army, cgsmediacomma-amc-dig-shared@mod uk, 2013. The British Army, Cyprus. Available at: www.army.mod.uk/operations-deployments/22728.aspx [accessed 16 November 2013].

6 Crossing borders, moving on

The urban music economy as a transformative realm

> I just wanted to make music; everything else is a bonus.
>
> (David, 27 – independent recording artist and business owner –
> interviewed in 2011)

In the UK, social mobility is at its lowest for decades. An individualised, market approach to inequality informs policies aiming to raise aspirations and improve the social mobility of young people from impoverished backgrounds. Yet for some, rendered almost invisible by a discourse about aspiration that is both classed and racialised, the urban music economy operates as a transformative realm. For young people from multicultural areas, participation in this sector allows for a metamorphosis into new identities. Within its remit, grime music embodies a cultural intermezzo where young people of Caribbean, African and English heritage work together; crossing borders and drawing on global and local influences to produce music that has an international reach (Back 1996, p. 4). It is evident that the creative and cultural industries are of growing economic significance. However, the urban music economy is an under-recognised constituent of this sector. As an occupational area, the creative and cultural industries are a desirable destination for large numbers of young people, yet they remain overwhelmingly white and middle class (CBI 2013; Neelands *et al.* 2015). An exploration of the workings of the grime music scene yields a partial but important view of the cultural dynamics of everyday life in a contemporary urban environment as young people find their own routes into a sector – the creative and cultural industries – that is effectively closed off to them.

Social policy development since the 1980s has been informed by a desire to reduce public expenditure, increase reliance on market forces and enhance consumer choice. Furthermore, the multicultural urban environment is being pushed towards an assimilation model where 'British values' tie us all together. This neo-liberal agenda makes it more difficult to talk about structural inequalities that are racialised, classed and gendered. In this climate, poverty is somehow the fault of the poor, created by a perceived cultural deficit in individuals from working-class and minority communities. At the intersection of class, ethnicity and poverty, it is ethnicity that continues to be a key signifier. For while there is a large diversity of fluid subject positions and cultural identities that constitute 'black', 'black youth' is posited generally as a problem category. The dominant representation of young black men as deviant, threatening and criminal is crisply demonstrated by the media response to the appointment, by the then Education Secretary Ed Balls, of MC Kano to promote the introduction of the new 14–18 diploma. Kano, a successful recording artist, was dismissed as 'a rapper famous for his violent and obscenity strewn lyrics' (Grimston 2010).

Kano, a long-time member of the grime music scene, is a young man who came of age in a multicultural urban environment: East Ham in the London borough of Newham. His scholastic journey makes him ideally placed to comment on the usefulness of vocational qualifications, yet this is ignored (Kano 2010). Although much has changed in the last thirty years in terms of how racial-ised practices are manifest and articulated, black cultural production still has little value. The sentiments in the recently released memo drafted by Oliver Letwin and Hartley Booth in 1985, in which they assert that riots were not caused by inequality and injustice but by individual characters with bad moral attitudes, gives a flavour of commonly held views at that time. In the same docu-ment, their insistence that any resources put in to these inner-city areas would only encourage 'new entrepreneurs [to] set up in the disco and drug trade' (Travis 2015) completely bypassed the crisis of unemployment in young black lives. Fast-forward three decades, and the lived experience of black youth, par-ticularly of those in urban settings, continues to involve the careful negotiation of the banal violence of quotidian microaggressions such as fewer job opportun-ities, heightened surveillance and increased levels of stop and search.

Social mobility and the creative and cultural industries

In the global north, the post-industrial city is on the rise, with a sharp polarisa-tion between the incomes of the elite and the working and workless poor. The poor are being actively displaced from the post-industrial city centre through socio-economic policy measures such as reduced housing benefits, rising housing costs and low wages. Post-World War II structural and economic changes saw the expansion and then the contraction of the state. From the 1970s, the labour market was routinely deregulated. In the 1980s and 1990s, the UK labour market underwent significant change, with a shift from a manufacturing to a more service-based economy and increased levels of part-time, temporary and less secure work. Furthermore, a drop in demand for unqualified 16-year-old school leavers was matched with a corresponding rise in the number of young people in full-time further education and training. Although the number of graduates has escalated considerably, the labour market has failed to meet the social demand for professional occupations, leading to what Brown calls 'social congestion', whereby a large number of young people are fighting to get into professions and willing to work for free to get a foot in the door (Brown 2013, p. 683). Be that as it may, young people from less privileged backgrounds are less able to do this.

In a neo-liberal landscape, high rates of social mobility are presumed to counter inequality. In 2009, the *Unleashing Aspirations* report issued by the Cabinet Office stated the necessity of a socially mobile society in order for the UK to flourish (Cabinet Office 2009). It asserted that the nation's global economic success depended on drawing on and utilising the talent in all sectors of the population. Two years later, the Conservative-led coalition government continued with this theme, producing a further report, *Opening Doors* (Cabinet Office 2011), which revealed that income and social class had a lasting impact on life chances; for example, while only 7 per cent of the population went to independent schools, the privately educated dominated the top level of most professions. It also found that social mobility had stalled and that patterns of advantage and disadvantage continued from one generation to the next.

Social mobility is a highly individualised outcome, and those who achieve it can move seamlessly through various spaces. Social immobility, on the other hand, particularly when it is perceived as a working-class attachment to place, has acquired connotations of defeat, fixity and failure (Allen and Hollingworth 2013, p. 500). Poverty of aspiration is seen as a barrier to social mobility; however, it is often couched as a model of deficit, in other words what young people from poor areas lack in terms of ambition, attitudes and behaviour that holds them back. But aspiration is a complex matter: it is not just in the mind; it is grounded in and bounded by material conditions and lived experiences. The market approach to social mobility assumes that competition forms the route to a fairer society, which means that those from disadvantaged backgrounds need only be given the opportunity to compete with the privileged.

The creative and cultural industries include TV, film, music, design, crafts, fashion, games and advertising. They are growing sectors that, according to some estimates, contribute 6 per cent of GDP, employ over two million people and grew by 9.9 per cent in 2013, faster than any other sector (CBI 2013; Neelands *et al.* 2015). In an increasingly global and digital economy, the creative and cultural industries are seen as a significant and influential mechanism to drive economic regeneration. In 2014, the gross value added (GVA) for the creative industries rose at a faster rate than did that for the financial services and construction sector. More people in the UK work in a creative role than in the NHS (GOV.UK 2014). And yet a recent major survey indicated that the creative and cultural industries continue to be a white, middle-class enclave (Create London 2015). This research also found that the majority of the respondents in the survey had at least one parent from a managerial or professional background, and more than half had a parent with a degree. Furthermore, the Creative Industries Federation report (2015) found that there was low diversity in the music sector, which tended to rely on graduates from socio-economically advantaged backgrounds for entry-level positions. Often these were positions that did not require a degree. Combine these findings with the fact that almost 90 per cent of the survey respondents had worked unpaid at some point in their career, and a desolate picture emerges in which young people without the necessary social, economic and cultural capital are unable to break into the creative and cultural industries. When all aspects of everyday life are translated into employability, young people are expected to capitalise on their networks and use these to access opportunities in employment. At the same time, it is more difficult for young people from less privileged backgrounds to find a way into creative work, particularly if they do not have access to, and are financially excluded from, internships and opportunities for unpaid work experience. I now turn to the urban music economy, a vibrant sector where young people who have been denied access to creative work generate work for themselves and others.

A transformative realm

Operating in the urban music economy provides moments for movement and transformation. As a nexus where class, ethnicity and poverty intersects, 'the ends', or poor neighbourhoods, are more often than not sites of advanced marginality (Wacquant 2007). The mechanisms to mobilise out of these environments are limited. In the past, perhaps, it was possible to use the acquisition of certain skills and qualifications as a method to climb the social ladder or acquire some spatial mobility. Now, however, social mobility is at a twenty-year low. A significant number of young people from poor areas still leave school without the required qualifications for entry into further education or other wider opportunities. In the UK, one of the wealthiest countries in the world, sizeable numbers of young people from poor backgrounds remain socially and economically immobile.

   Creating music and its by-products allows young people, many of whom are young black men, to cross borders. This border crossing is between genres, roles, locations and identities. According to Vieira, individuals have a desire to seek other shores, and identity is constructed and reconstructed as we transit from one bank to another (Vieira 2014). Although reconstructing identities is a complex process in which social groups and lived experiences play their part, what lies between these banks, for most people, is the potential for possibility and opportunity. Participating in the urban music economy enabled the majority of my respondents to seek and find other shores, leaving their everyday environment for a more far-reaching experience of life in the UK and beyond. In so doing, their identities are transformed. James talked about growing up in inner-city London and travelling to places such as Amsterdam, Croatia and Cyprus through his activities in the urban music sector. It had heightened his awareness of the paucity of his surroundings and contributed to his understanding of how the world works, or 'knowing my way around':

> Ah, I think, … I wouldn't say they are the best of areas, but I don't know, you don't learn that until you get older and you branch out and see other places and you realise it's not as nice as other areas. Yeah, I think that DJ'ing played a big part in seeing loads of other places, definitely, knowing my way around, like.
>
> (James, 25 – club and radio DJ – interviewed in 2008)

For Brian, a twenty-year veteran in the urban music sector, there was an unspoken sense of pride when he listed some of the countries that he had worked in: 'I play in the UK, been to Serbia, play in Switzerland, Italy, Paris, south of France' (Brian, 40 – club and radio DJ – interviewed in 2009).

What lies at the heart of creativity is redefinition, or the ability to take something and make or remake it anew. It is within this context that the grime music scene and the wider urban music economy operates as a transformative realm. For some years, grime has had a global reach that includes Japan, Croatia, Canada and now the United States. Grime music does not fit neatly into national borders and, wherever it is found in the world, it retains its specific and distinct sound. Grime evolved from the UK garage scene, and, because of its turbulent reputation, the authorities remained anxious about how to control it. Live performance of grime music became problematic, and events were often shut down. A blog entry on MySpace in 2006 bemoans the number of garage and grime events that had been cancelled or shut down during the preceding six years (The Grime Report 2006). Hancox (2010) and Izundu (2010) provide examples of how events were often cancelled due to a perceived threat of trouble.

However, unlike its predecessor garage, grime did not fade away. Instead, advances in technology enabled performance of this creative expression to disseminate outwards from inner London, establishing audiences in the surrounding counties and across the UK. The Sidewinder events in Swindon illustrate this (Sidewinder 2006). Also in Europe in 2007, grime DJs Spyro and DJ Mak 10 played UK funky on Nissi Beach in Ayia Napa, Cyprus (SelectaLimit 2007), in North America – Wiley's radio set in Toronto was one of many he conducted that year (ninkyrooz 2013) and, in 2009, Marcus Nasty discussed his experience of performing in the Gambia (Clark 2009). It is this international dimension that is in evidence when, in 2007, Jay-Z rapped over Lethal Bizzle's iconic grime track *Pow* (queenofclubz 2006). Furthermore, in the opinion of many commentators, grime has experienced something of a resurgence in the last two years. Some key markers and events from 2014 and 2015 include *German Whip*, by Meridian Dan, a recording that was initially promoted entirely online via social media and YouTube. *German Whip* got to number 13 in the UK national chart in May 2014. To date, the video has just under six million views on YouTube (via SBTV) and a further 1.9 million on Vevo (MeridianDanVEVO 2014). Also, in February 2015, when Kanye West performed at the Brits, he brought approximately twenty UK grime artists, including Skepta, JME, Novelist (Kojo Kankam), Stormzy and Wiley, on stage with him. Later in the year, Canadian artist Drake invited Skepta to perform with him at the Wireless Festival in London. Stormzy (Michael Omari) and Wretch 32 (Jermaine Sinclair) performed with the London Philharmonic Orchestra at the Royal Albert Hall in August. In December 2015, south London grime MC Stormzy achieved a higher position in the national charts than the X Factor winner, with a track *Shut Up* promoted almost exclusively through a Twitter campaign. Likewise, in December, Reuben Dangoor's portraits of grime artists were displayed at the Tate Gallery (Tate Britain 2015). Although, from these exertions, it might appear that grime 'made a comeback', in truth, it never went away: it has been a key component of the urban music economy for more than a decade.

In his black Atlantic trope, Paul Gilroy suggests that movement, transformation and relocation are intrinsic factors in the creation of black identities (Gilroy 1996). This concept can be used for a complex reading of the black male experience as it pertains to the urban music industry. The trajectory of DJ Marcus Nasty illustrates this point well, as he has reinvented himself within and outside of genres (grime, UK funky and bass) and roles (DJ, talent scout and event promoter).

Marcus Nasty, a former leader of a grime crew, is now a sought-after DJ in the urban music economy. His transformation is foregrounded here because his transcendence of boundaries is one of the most marked. In his own words, he became a DJ because 'he'd been away for a while ... and when he came back he wanted something to do' (Sigel 2011). His early reputation is tied up with the more difficult aspects of grime and its discontents. An unintended consequence of the disciplinary techniques that the grime scene was subjected to was the creation of more broad-based audiences as well as an opportunity for participants to navigate out of their local environment. Marcus Nasty, however, had to find a different route because the combination of his reputation and the perception of the grime music scene as a volatile and potentially dangerous creative expression meant that he was subjected to the many disciplinary procedures that organise

Figure 6.1 DJ Marcus Nasty, Stormin and MC Shantie playing and performing UK funky in the heart of Shoreditch in 2008. Marcus Nasty was a founder member of N.A.S.T.Y crew. Stormin, formerly a grime MC, is now a stalwart in the drum and bass scene.

social space (Stanley-Niaah 2004). Therefore, as many of these avenues were closed off or severely curtailed, he continued to scout talent for N.A.S.T.Y crew and, as a new music scene – UK funky – began to emerge, he found his metier in increasing participation in this scene. In an interview with an online magazine in 2009, he describes growing up with a father who was a musician, how he eventually became a DJ and his subsequent transition from being a founder of N.A.S.T.Y crew to playing UK funky: 'My name was quite messy before, and I'm not trying to be that person anymore'. At one point, he became so associated with the UK funky scene in Ayia Napa that for a while he was known as Marcus 'Ayia Napa' Nasty. Ayia Napa, in Cyprus, hosts a specific and particular audience from the UK. This audience comes to participate in a music scene that has been momentarily transplanted from an urban environment to a marketplace that has been created through the entrepreneurial activities of young men of Caribbean descent. It is a long way from the street corners and council estates in east London, where Marcus Nasty and so many artist-entrepreneurs like him established their ground. Marcus Nasty is a pioneer in three key genres in the urban music economy: grime, UK funky and bass. His 2013 performance at the Snowbombing Festival in Austria temporarily locates him in a world that is far removed from 'the ends' and clandestine pirate radio broadcasts.[1]

Transformation through commodification

Over the last century there has been a transformation from a society of producers to a society of consumers (Bauman 2007). This is apparent in all markets, including the music industry. The ecology of the urban music economy is formed out of a complex series of interactions with and between practitioners and their environment. It is a repository for a multiplicity of interconnected activities. As a constituent component of the popular music industry, this economy has benefited from the technological advances of the last decade. The recorded music industry is dominated by three record companies: Universal Music Group, Sony Music Entertainment and Warner Music Group, commonly known as the 'Big Three' (previously, before mergers, the 'Big Four'). In the twenty-first century, the Internet has allowed artists in the urban music economy to transcend distance and reach large audiences without the intervention of these 'Big Three'. A space has been created in which UK urban music artists can achieve creative acclaim and economic success. Urban music artists create and sell online personas in exchange for recognition and feedback. It is entirely possible for independent recording artists in the urban music economy to establish a fan base through having an online presence. JME, for example, has almost half a million followers on Twitter, and his Twitter profile indicates his willingness to act as his own salesperson, when he states that he has: 'No label, No PR, No manager' (JmeVerified account 2008).

As a commodified cultural practice, there is a seamless integration between culture and commerce, and many participants in the urban music economy promote themselves as a branded product 'using the best means at their disposal to enhance the market value of the goods they sell' (Bauman 2007, p. 6). The means at their disposal include social media and online and digital TV channels. A cursory glance at the Twitter and Instagram profiles of an aspiring artist will quickly reveal links to merchandise for sale, promotional details and booking processes. For urban music practitioners 'turning into a desirable and desired commodity is the stuff of which dreams and fairytales are made' (Bauman 2007, p. 13) and, I would suggest, nightmares. The road to commodification is littered with stories of artists being discarded by a notoriously fickle industry in which an artist rapidly becomes outdated and unfit for further use.

While it is perceived to be a taste that is acquired by young people from impoverished backgrounds, grime has little value as creative practice. That is until it finds a broader audience in the mainstream. Then a flurry of activity takes place to bring these artists under the auspices of the formal recorded music industry. Between 2007 and 2010, a steady number of grime MCs were signed by one of the 'Big Four' record labels, but these arrangements were, for the most part, short-lived. For example, Scorcher – signed and then released by Geffen – continues to release music independently (see *Rockstar*). Scorcher also appeared in the first series of UK television drama Top Boy, along with Ashley Walters (Asher D), formerly of So Solid Crew, and Kane Robinson (Kano), former member of N.A.S.T.Y crew. In addition, the following artists were signed and then departed from major labels: Chipmunk (Jahmaal Fyfe) to Columbia Sony, Griminal to Universal and Devlin to Island. All continue as independent recording artists. Although these artists are getting by on their own terms, recording and releasing music, travelling extensively and establishing concurrent careers, the Big Four experience can be damaging, as evidenced by Chipmunk's recently released track *Sonic Boom*, in which he talks about the industry 'chewing him up and spitting him out'.

Many grime MCs were 'shelved' after a perceived lack of commercial success, including Chipmunk. What does it do to you as an individual to be picked up and then cast aside, to become the collateral damage, if you like, of a society of consumers? David, whose quote opens this chapter, talked about 'everything else' being a 'bonus', the 'everything else' being the income that comes from the sale of merchandise (T-shirts and caps); the 'bonus', the opportunity to make a living.

New identities

In the urban music economy, of which grime is an integral part, we see a 'politics which works with and through difference' (Hall 1992, p. 252) where there is a dual identification of being from dense urban settings while reaching into diaspora cultural heritage. These new identities engage with difference, but they are contingent, as is illustrated by Dappy's recent skirmish with the use of the N-word in his freestyle *Tarzan 3*. Interestingly, Dappy, formerly of N-Dubz, a north London artist of Greek-Cypriot heritage, had just as much vitriol heaped on him for saying that 'we' reclaimed the word as he had for using the N-word itself. By way of explanation, he stated that the 'we' did not mean he was saying he was black, rather it included anyone from the inner city or a council estate (BBC Newsbeat 2015).

Nevertheless, young people involved in the grime scene are, for the most part, of Caribbean and African descent. Grime allows us to see and imagine new types of association and, in many ways, grime can be seen as a cultural intermezzo where new identities are possible (up to a point − there are limits and borders). Contemporary black experience is one of diaspora − a process of unsettling, recombination and hybridisation (Hall 1992, p. 258). Diaspora experience of the grime scene is nourished by connections with the Caribbean, particularly Jamaican dancehall (see Krept and Konan *Freak of the Week* and Chipmunk and Mavado *Every Gal*) and, in 2012 Skepta − an independent recording artist of Nigerian descent − went to Jamaica to prepare for the Red Bull Culture Clash. Accompanied by members of the Boy Better Know (BBK) crew, including Shorty, Jammer, Frisco, Solo 45, Lazy and DJ Maximum, BBK travelled to Kingston to immerse themselves in sound system culture. Skepta described meeting artists such as U-Roy, Ricky Trooper and Popcaan as 'the originators, masters and legends of what we do' (Red Bull Music Academy 2014).

Two years later, in 2014, the subsequent Red Bull Culture Clash continued this black Atlantic flow when it was streamed live online from London. BBK, Rebel Sound (a collaboration between David Rodigan, Shy FX and Chase and Status), A$AP Mob from the US (but including A$AP Ferg, who is of Caribbean heritage) and Jamaican sound system Stone Love competed in a sound clash in Earls Court. In December 2015, JME and his brother Skepta went to Lagos with Stormzy and south London duo Krept and Konan (Casyo Johnson and Karl Wilson respectively) for the Beat FM Christmas concert. Krept and Konan are of Caribbean heritage. A local newspaper report stated that: 'The South London rapper, Stormzy, announced on stage that he was of Ghanaian descent' at the event, which also included performances from Nigerian artists Falz, Phyno and Olamide.

For Stuart Hall, 'black' was a way to reference common experiences of racism, a singular unifying identity across ethnic and cultural differences at a time when black experience was placed at the margins (Hall 1992, p. 252). However, black in the context of the urban music economy means to be Caribbean and to be African, particularly west African. Furthermore, new identities, produced in part through a productive tension between local and global influences, means that being English (white or black) is also an intrinsic component of this cultural intermezzo (Back 1996, p. 4). These identities are contingent and fluid; for example, Stormzy is an English MC in the UK but introduces himself as Ghanaian at the Christmas concert in Lagos. Likewise Skepta is Nigerian in Lagos and an English MC in New York. And Wiley, deported from Canada to Glasgow in 2014, faced the cultural confusion when presented with a Scottish 'square sausage' (FACTmagazine 2014). Moreover, Wiley walked off stage at the Cockrock festival in Cumbria after ten minutes, citing a health and safety issue, but in a post-event commentary on Twitter, the east Londoner from Bow stated: 'Please stop sending me to farms to perform, I'm a yardie man' (Gibsone 2013). And lastly, Logan Sama, a white DJ and another long-time player in the grime scene, who started out on pirate radio with a three-year stint on Rinse FM before moving to Kiss FM for ten years, recently had to defend his authority to comment on grime after he caused a minor furore on Twitter by stating that grime was not solely black music (Logan Sama 2015). These accounts bring to the fore the 'new and challenging forms of cultural practice and identity formation that have been produced in a metropolitan context' (Back 1996, p. 3) where young people can simultaneously perform identities that are urban, London, Caribbean, English and African.

Grime as a black vernacular neo-liberal paradox

Today, neo-liberalism has become common sense. Increasingly, what is valued is the attitude of the 'striver' with 'self-belief' and 'dream, believe, achieve' dispensed as common tropes. The prevailing view that societal ills can be overcome by individual hard work has replaced notions of community responsibility. I spoke to George in 2009 and Andrew in 2008:

> I think that you can only get there by working hard, and working with as many people as possible that are willing to work with me, working hard, doing a big portfolio, and hopefully one day ... to the top.
>
> (George, 24 – music producer – interviewed in 2009)

> I could round it up to say I am just going be rich and successful (laughs). Yeah, just want to make good music, you know show people from my area and other areas and abroad that, no matter where you're from you can do whatever you like if you have the right mind.
>
> (Andrew, 18 – MC/recording artist – interviewed in 2008)

Both of these young men were from modest backgrounds and trying to find a place for themselves through hard work and individual self-realisation. In many ways, this is the legacy of Thatcher and Blair. Structural inequalities, including racism, were not articulated as a barrier to success, even among those, such as Colin, who had been the furthest from the labour market:

> I've got a lot of links. I'm establishing myself in the industry as a music producer. It's not about race or anything; it's about using your talents the best you can. The way I saw it, I had two options. I came from a bad situation and I was away for a long time in that situation. I had two choices: I could actually go get myself a job that I didn't want or I could stay in my room and believe in a dream that was looking so dark from where I've come from. And I think to myself, ok, what can I do? I pursued music, I stayed in my room for a year and made music.
>
> (Colin, 24 – music producer – interviewed in 2010)

It would seem that those who have bought into an individualised, market approach are those who have the least to gain (Gilroy 2013, p. 25). Chipmunk, the north London MC, has 'believe, achieve' inscribed in ink on his body, while for Jamal Edwards 'self-belief' replaces 'smokey barz' as the motto for SBTV, the online TV channel he set up as a sixteen-year-old. In other words the belief persists that, as Gilroy argues, 'anyone can change their circumstances by sheer dedicated force of will' (Gilroy 2013, p. 26). And yet collaborative, partnership working is a crucial practice in the urban music sector. Wiley recently tweeted a stream of advice to up-and-coming artists, effectively telling them that if they have a modicum of success as an independent, not to sign that freedom away on a contract with a record label. Social media sites are awash with tales of striving harder to make success happen. A minority voice is Keith Dube – who writes as Mr Exposed – who offers a rare critique of an unthinking following of the 'hard work brings rewards mantra' from a perspective of 'the ends' (Dube 2016).

Conclusion

The rapidly changing topography of the urban music economy is difficult to capture; however, this chapter provides a snapshot of how the scene works. Against a backdrop of declining social mobility and rising youth unemployment, the transformative aspects of the sector take on a deep significance. A glance back to the 1970s reveals the motifs of an economic crisis: stagflation, increasing oil and energy prices, and a three-day week. The subsequent political era ushered in a neo-liberal agenda that identified the 'welfare state' as part of the problem that had led to the economic downturn. Mass unemployment in the late 1970s and early 1980s had a critical effect on young people who as a result experienced wage scarring and limited opportunities. The subsequent dismantling and privatisation of state functions has had an enduring negative impact on young people from poor backgrounds. Since then, structural changes in the UK economy have disrupted the school-to-work and education-to-employment transitions. Whereas in the post-World War II era the majority of young people left school at the end of secondary schooling, now an increasing number stay beyond the compulsory school leaving age. When Tony Blair launched Labour's education manifesto in 2001, he outlined a target that 50 per cent of those aged 18–30 would attend university (BBC News 2002). Subsequently, under the guise of 'widening participation' in higher education, large numbers of young people from poor backgrounds were encouraged to pursue credentials. They are now mired in debt. The increased access to good quality work and better life chances promised them have not been forthcoming.

The austerity measures implemented by the coalition in 2010 and continued by the current Conservative government as a response to the global economic downturn in 2008 have not ceased. Ongoing cuts to public services have resulted in the decimation of youth provision. Youth centres and places to gather in the community are a thing of the past. In this landscape, young people, particularly the urban poor, are rendered out of time and out of place. As public locations in which to congregate disappear, the opportunity for physical contact lessens, and the world becomes a smaller place. Furthermore, the gentrification of urban areas and the closure of increasing numbers of live music venues puts pressure on a scene that relies on public performance as a way to make a living. Despite this retrenchment, the enterprising pursuits of artist-entrepreneurs in inner-city areas have enabled the creation of national and global markets and performance spaces.

The creative and cultural industries are a significant sector for economic growth and ought to provide opportunities for young people who have the necessary skills, interests and talents to earn a living. But this sector has some of the lowest diversity rates in terms of ethnicity and class. For young people from poor backgrounds, education used to be a mechanism for social mobility; however, this is no longer the case. For those with few qualifications, even entry-level employment is difficult to obtain. Recent studies also show that black graduates are less likely to be employed (Zwysen and Longhi 2016) and that when black and ethnic minority workers are employed, they earn less than their white counterparts. This is the case in any occupational sector, regardless of qualifications (TUC 2016). Self-employment is often touted as a way out of insecure job prospects, but self-employment itself can be a mask for financial precariousness, as workers, particularly in the creative sectors, struggle to make a living.

Although the urban music economy is an under-acknowledged segment within the creative and cultural industries, it has a global reach and provides job and career opportunities to people who are, on the whole, cast out of the sector. In the UK, black cultural production still appears to have little value, even though its practitioners have internationally recognised skills as recording artists, DJs, film-makers, sound engineers and music producers. Passion and agency in creative work and the project-based nature of creative employment give workers in the urban music economy an opportunity to exercise agency over their working lives (Umney and Kretsos 2015, p. 317).

The post-World War II black settlement in the UK was characterised by a tentative welcome that soon turned to anti-black discrimination. The subsequent political resistance and civil uprising gave way to the multiculturalism that is the lived experience of practitioners in the urban music sector. Young people lack (or refuse) a historic engagement with this political past. The volatile racial politics of the 1970s and 1980s appear to have little significance for cultural production in this economy. Whereas in past decades it was possible to identify as 'black' due to a common experience of racism, it is no longer possible to mobilise around a totalising 'black experience' as a singular and unifying framework (although it is still a desirable outcome for those former DJs in the urban music economy who seek to commodify an essentialised black history). Once a powerful symbol of black unity in the 1980s, the colour combination of red, gold and green is now a rare sight in young lives. Nevertheless, in the given names of urban music artists Jammer and Chipmunk (Jahmek Power and Jahmaal Fyfe respectively), it is possible to see the traces of a black political narrative that references Rastafarian ideals. It is also evident that in the past black music had a different value, operating as a paid-for product but also as a connection to shared history and heritage. However, the opening years of the twenty-first century have seen the emergence of a commercial urban black aesthetic that has subsumed a politics of black identity. At the same time, participants in the urban music economy have a powerful sense of themselves as agents on a national and sometimes international scale.

In crews and other peer groups, artist-entrepreneurs in the urban music economy establish kinship networks that are supportive, nurturing and nourishing. The music they create connects to a diaspora heritage even if the practitioners, as individuals, do not readily make the historical links to it in the same way. The disparity in how these cultural identities are articulated may depend on the proximity to the cultural source, and whether that source is African or Caribbean and whether the connection comes via a grandparent or a parent. While black cultural identities challenge the notion that British culture is essentially white, new racisms mean that white audiences can enjoy unrestricted access to black cultural forms, such as grime, in a way that black youth cannot.

I have shown how participation in urban music economy allows for a distinct formulation of spatial and social mobility. This movement is a continuous process. It enables transformation to take place and it allows for a shift away from categories and identifications such as 'socially excluded' that are imprecise and potentially damaging. The impact and significance of grime and other urban music genres have been rendered almost invisible because they are the creative practice of the urban poor. To succeed in this economy, young people must turn themselves into a commodity. Although this commodification offers opportunities to earn a living, artists can suffer a singular existential crisis when their brand loses its allure. Accessible technologies mean that practitioners can simultaneously experience the world both as a cellular, personal construct and as a global aspect. The participants in this economy may have fewer restrictions in terms of postcode battles and turf wars, but because all private life is lived publicly, every aspect of daily life is subject to comment, and that in turn intensifies vulnerability and affects emotional well-being. While buying into the neo-liberal dream of individual responsibility for success, public failure is compounded by racism and disadvantage. The damage to self that comes from playing this version of the game is delicately balanced against the liberating effect of making it on one's own terms. These are young people who refuse to be carved out of the opportunities for desirable work in the creative sector.

My respondents were mainly of Caribbean and African heritage living side by side with their English peers in dense urban settings. Most did not articulate the impact of structural inequalities and historical injustice that pervaded their everyday lives. This is not to say that they were unaware of the limits and borders placed around their lives; rather, the preferred mode of seeing and operating in the world was one of working harder to achieve their goals. On the whole, these were young black men who had produced value for themselves despite the negative attributes of their social positioning. And therein lies the most fundamental incongruence: creating grime and other genres in the urban music economy is a highly individualised practice that relies on sharing skills, knowledge and resources. Nevertheless, this cannot obscure the fact that operating in this sector enables young black men, in particular, to cross borders, make new identities and land on different shores.

Note

1 In an interview to mark eighteen years of Rinse FM, formerly a pirate radio station, Marcus Nasty describes sneaking out of his house as a school-age teenager to be at the radio station, which was at one point broadcasting from a tree house on the A12.

References

Allen, K. and Hollingworth, S., 2013. 'Sticky subjects' or 'cosmopolitan creatives'? Social class, place and urban young people's aspirations for work in the knowledge economy. *Urban Studies*, 50(3), pp. 499–517.

Back, L., 1996. *New ethnicities and urban culture*, UCL Press. Available at: https://books.google.co.uk/books/about/New_Ethnicities_and_Urban_Culture.html?id=m W906f1B9zkC [accessed 14 January 2016].

Bauman, Z., 2007. *Consuming life*, Cambridge, UK and Malden, MA: Polity Press.

BBC News, 2002. Blair's university targets spelt out. *BBC*. Available at: http://news.bbc.co.uk/1/hi/education/1789500.stm [accessed 18 April 2016].

BBC Newsbeat, 2015. N-Dubz rapper Dappy defends use of n-word in new song. Available at: www.bbc.co.uk/newsbeat/article/35194389/n-dubz-rapper-dappy-defends-use-of-n-word-in-new-song [accessed 28 February 2016].

Brown, P., 2013. Education, opportunity and the prospects for social mobility. *British Journal of Sociology of Education*, 34(5–6), pp. 678–700.

Cabinet Office, 2009. *Unleashing aspiration: The final report of the panel on fair access to the profession.*

Cabinet Office, 2011. *Opening doors, breaking barriers: A strategy for social mobility.*

CBI, 2013. CBI: Creative industries: One of the fastest growing sectors in the UK. Available at: www.cbi.org.uk/business-issues/creative-industries/ [accessed 22 June 2013].

Clark, M., 2009. Blackdown: Marcus NASTY interview. *Blackdown*. Available at: http://blackdownsoundboy.blogspot.com/2009/09/marcus-nasty-interview.html [accessed 27 July 2011].

Create London, 2015. Survey: Panic. Available at: www.createlondon.org/panic/survey/ [accessed 27 February 2016].

Creative Industries Federation, 2015. *Creative diversity: The state of diversity in the UK's creative industries, and what we can do about it.*, London: Creative Industries Federation.

Dube, K., 2016. Keith Dube. Available at: http://keithdube.co/ [accessed 28 February 2016].

FACTmagazine, 2014. Wiley gets deported from Canada, explodes all over Twitter. *FACT Magazine: Music News, New Music*. Available at: www.factmag.com/2014/04/03/wiley-gets-deported-from-canada-explodes-all-over-twitter/ [accessed 27 February 2016].

Gibsone, H., 2013. Wiley walks off stage at Cockrock festival, calls audience 'pagans'. *Guardian*. Available at: www.theguardian.com/music/2013/jul/22/wiley-cockrock-festival-pagans [accessed 24 December 2015].

Gilroy, P., 1996. *The Black Atlantic*, London: Verso.

Gilroy, P., 2013. '…We got to get over before we go under…': Fragments for a history of black vernacular neoliberalism. *New Formations*, (80/81).

GOV.UK, 2014. Creative Industries worth £8million an hour to UK economy. Available at: www.gov.uk/government/news/creative-industries-worth-8million-an-hour-to-uk-economy [accessed 28 February 2016].

Grimston, J., 2010. Foul-mouthed rapper Kano helps Ed Balls to promote school diplomas. Available at: http://journalisted.com/article/18mg3 [accessed 28 February 2016].

Hall, S., 1992. New ethnicities. In J. Donald and A. Rattansi, eds. *Race, culture and difference*. London and Newbury Park, CA: Sage Publications.

Hancox, D., 2010. Grime: Banished from physical London. Available at: http://danhancox.blogspot.co.uk/2010/02/grime-banished-from-physical-london.html [accessed 16 June 2013].

Izundu, C.C., 2010. Police defend club check forms. *BBC*. Available at: www.bbc.co.uk/newsbeat/10174673 [accessed 16 June 2013].

JmeVerified account, 2008. Jme (@JmeBBK). *Twitter*. Available at: https://twitter.com/JmeBBK [accessed 8 February 2015].

Kano, 2010. Kano: I'm helping the future of our youth. *Guardian*. Available at: www.theguardian.com/music/musicblog/2010/jan/15/kano-future-youth [accessed 28 February 2016].

Logan Sama, 2015. Logan Sama on Twitter. *Twitter*. Available at: https://twitter.com/djlogansama/status/679004624762851329 [Accessed 28 February 2016].

MeridianDanVEVO, 2014. *Meridian Dan: German Whip*. Available at: www.youtube.com/watch?v=HNnrW54xPaY&feature=youtube_gdata_player [accessed 8 February 2015].

Neelands, J., Belfiore, E., Firth, C., Hart, N., Perrin, L., Brock, S., Holdaway, D. and Woddis, J., 2015. *Enriching Britain: Culture, creativity and growth*, University of Warwick.

ninkyrooz, 2013. *Wiley & Freeza Chin (radio set in Toronto) 2013 new !!!!! Bigggg!!*. Available at: www.youtube.com/watch?v=ZLDJl0dibPo&feature=youtube_gdata_player [accessed 8 February 2015].

queenofclubz, 2006. *Jay-Z over Lethal B Pow*. Available at: www.youtube.com/watch?v=QMuc7wgdokY&feature=youtube_gdata_player [accessed 5 July 2013].

Red Bull Music Academy, 2014. Film: Boy Better Know in Jamaica. *Red Bull Music Academy Daily*. Available at: http://daily.redbullmusicacademy.com/2014/09/boy-better-know-in-jamaica-film [accessed 28 February 2016].

SelectaLimit, 2007. *Dj Spyro and Dj Mak 10 B2B Napa Nissi Beach*. Available at: www.youtube.com/watch?v=Dmq8mSSVZHo&feature=youtube_gdata_player [accessed 5 February 2011].

Sidewinder, 2006. Sidewinder, Tommorow Night! Brunel Rooms, Swindon!! ITS GRIII-IME. Available at: www.hijackbristol.co.uk/board/the-forum/sidewinder-tommorow-night!-brunel-rooms-swindon!!-its-griiiime/?wap2 [accessed 16 November 2013].

Sigel, T., 2011. Marcus Nasty talks about the hunger it took to get on #DECA10 [VIDEO] RWD: The UK's biggest and best youth lifestyle title; fashion, games, events, gadgets, music and more. Available at: www.rwdmag.com/2011/09/marcus-nasty-talks-about-the-hunger-it-took-to-get-on-deca10-video [accessed 22 September 2011].

Stanley-Niaah, S., 2004. Kingston's dancehall: A story of space and celebration. *Space and Culture*, 7(1), pp. 102–118.

Tate Britain, 2015. Late at Tate Britain: Celebrity. Available at: www.tate.org.uk/whats-on/tate-britain/performance-and-music/late-tate-britain-celebrity [accessed 28 February 2016].

The Grime Report, 2006. The Grime Report [Webzine] on Myspace. *Myspace*. Available at: www.myspace.com/thegrimereport/blog/128694899 [accessed 14 April 2012].

Travis, A., 2015. Oliver Letwin blocked help for black youth after 1985 riots. *The Guardian*. Available at: www.theguardian.com/politics/2015/dec/30/oliver-letwin-blocked-help-for-black-youth-after-1985-riots [accessed 27 February 2016].

TUC, 2016. BAME workers with degrees two and half times more likely to be unemployed, finds TUC. *TUC*. Available at: www.tuc.org.uk/equality-issues/black-workers/labour-market/bame-workers-degrees-two-and-half-times-more-likely-be [accessed 16 April 2016].

Umney, C. and Kretsos, L., 2015. 'That's the experience': Passion, work precarity, and life transitions among London jazz musicians. *Work and Occupations* 42(3), pp. 313–334.

Vieira, R., 2014. Life stories, cultural métissage, and personal identities. *SAGE Open*, 4(1). Available at: http://sgo.sagepub.com/content/4/1/2158244013517241.abstract.

Wacquant, L., 2007. *Urban outcasts: A comparative sociology of advanced marginality*, Cambridge, UK: Polity.

Zwysen, W. and Longhi, S., 2016. Black workers' pay gap in UK 'widens with qualifications'. Colchester, UK: Institute for Social and Economic Research. Available at: www.iser.essex.ac.uk/research/publications/523474 [accessed 18 April 2016].

Part IV
Conclusion

7 The wrap up

Entrepreneurship in the urban music economy

> From that point twenty years ago, ... the journey has been tremendous. It has taken us around the world, taken us into areas we maybe wouldn't have been able to get into and managed to keep us out of trouble to a degree.
>
> (Fred, 40 – DJ and event promoter – interviewed in 2009)

The quote that opens this concluding chapter comes from Fred, who was reflecting on the opportunities that two decades of work in the urban music economy had afforded him. Fred has resisted full participation in the formal economy. For twenty years he has eked out a living on pirate radio and in clubs as a DJ, enjoying a somewhat precarious autonomy. While Fred is a veteran in this sector, it is also an arena for younger participants. I began this book by looking at the achievements of Dizzee Rascal, an 18-year-old man who, at the time he won the Mercury Music Prize, asserted that he 'came from nothing' (BBC News Channel 2003). In fact, his 'nothing' was a location in London, one of the richest cities in the world. Dizzee Rascal hails from Tower Hamlets, a district, little more than two miles from London's financial heart, that still contains areas of deep poverty. His other 'nothing' was the experience of regular exclusions from secondary school and then leaving with few qualifications. In inner-city east London, which was my entry point to this study, at different levels on the scale, there are many more young people like him without the necessary accreditations for transition into adult life. Despite being host boroughs for the London 2012 Olympics, Newham, Hackney and Tower Hamlets were, until relatively recently, the three most deprived boroughs in London (HM Government 2007). Although wealthier residents have moved into these areas, a recent study indicates that 40 per cent of households earned less that 60 per cent of the national median income[1] (Hanna and Bosetti 2015). Over the last two decades, there has been regeneration and redevelopment on a significant scale, including the extension of the Jubilee Line to Stratford in 1999 and the opening of Westfield, the third largest shopping centre in the UK. However, urban east London still has as many betting shops as banks, and social, economic and financial exclusion remains entrenched. London, as a city, remains divided according to money and wealth. While Dizzee Rascal has gone on to achieve critical acclaim and financial success as a grime MC, there are other untold stories, narratives of resistance and resilience where self-confessed 'troubled kids' like my informant Adam claim a space in which they can also become successful on their own terms.

Because educational achievement, particularly the acquisition of qualifications, is deemed to be so important for personal and national success, underachievement is a problem that cannot be left unfixed. A Centre for Analysis of Social Exclusion (CASE) report in 1999 highlighted a clear link between low attainment, truancy, school exclusion and crime (Sparkes 1999). More recent research shows that this connection still exists (Children's Commissioner 2013). Therefore educating and training young people to the highest levels will enable them to face an uncertain globalised future, particularly because workers with low qualifications have a reduced chance of permanent, stable employment (du Bois-Reymond 2004, p. 7; Leitch 2006; Communities and Local Government 2007; Sergeant 2009b).

Entrepreneurship is seen as a significant factor for economic growth and all the more important as the developed world endeavours to pull itself out of an acute global recession. It is almost a given that individuals with entrepreneurial behaviours are vital for economic success. This focus on enterprise as a key tenet for economic recovery is manifest through the UK policy to develop entrepreneurship skills and attributes among young people through the implementation of enterprise education in primary and secondary schools and the mandatory work experience for those aged fifteen and sixteen (Schoof 2006; Ofsted 2011).

Enterprise education, which aims to increase employability and encourage young people to become entrepreneurs, suggests that those who receive enterprise education acquire a more entrepreneurial outlook and are more likely to think about running their own business (Department for Children, Schools and Families 2010; Wicks 2013). The Start Up loan scheme (Start Up Loans 2013), created in 2012 by the Department for Business, Innovation and Skills to support young people who have a feasible business idea, and the Prince's Trust, who offer low-interest loans and mentoring (Prince's Trust Enterprise Programme 2014), are examples of initiatives to support business start-up by young people.

The Future Jobs Fund (FJF), another policy response to rising levels of youth unemployment and increased numbers of NEETs formed part of the Young Persons Guarantee, a Labour government action started in 2009 and shelved by the coalition government in 2010 (Directgov 2011). FJF mandated those who had been in receipt of Jobseekers Allowance for six months or more to take a job on at least the national minimum wage, with sanctions such as the removal of benefit if they refused. The wages for those on the FJF programme were paid by the state. The coalition government replaced the FJF scheme with the Youth Contract as a new response to rising youth unemployment. These measures included

160,000 Government-subsidised jobs; an extra 250,000 work experience places; extra financial incentives for employers to take on apprentices;

additional support for young unemployed people through Jobcentre Plus; and a new payment-by-results initiative focused on 16–17 year olds with no qualifications.

(UK Parliament 2012)

Again, these measures assume that those who are NEET have little work experience and require vocational qualifications to secure jobs. However, I have shown through my research that measures to tackle the NEET issue will not have the desired outcomes if there is a continued misrecognition and misunderstanding regarding the activities that young people, categorised as NEET, are actually engaged in.

The informal economy may be viewed as something that needs to be eradicated or brought into line because its existence is seen to be unfair to those who adhere to the legal and state requirements (Grabiner 2000), but through my research I have shown that operating in this sector allows business and enterprise to be created. The informal economy is assumed to be fragmented and unregulated, leaving those that participate in it at risk of exploitation; however, I found that in the urban music economy, participants are subjected to the same level of regulation – including licensing and health and safety – whether they operate in the formal or informal sector. Also, the changing nature of work in the formal sector, with, for example, zero-hours contracts and other employment structures that offer few benefits, means that the formal sector can be just as insecure and unstructured as the informal sector (Williams and Nadin 2012). The simultaneous occupation of the formal and informal spheres allows for the creation of self-employment in areas of advanced marginality where there is high and persistent unemployment. Economic advance and strategies to reduce youth unemployment therefore need to include discussion on the informal sector. A pick-and-mix approach to employment for young people would enable a move back and forth and in between both sectors, particularly in terms of establishing enterprise.

Four key themes emerge from this book: first, how the identification of being NEET obscures the significant and valuable achievements of young people from poor areas generally and young black men in particular; second, how grime is used as a lens to disrupt the definition of what it means to be NEET and to draw attention to the socio-economic and cultural importance of a thus far underresearched area, the urban music economy; third, how narratives of resistance and resilience have been developed through enterprise; and finally, how a passion for music and its related enterprise has determined a new reality that transcends everyday tropes of failure and underachievement.

The NEET category

The NEET category that a sizeable number of young people are placed in is a category of deficit. In other words, those classified thus are neither working nor learning. It implies inactivity and immobility. Within this category, individuals are distributed 'along a scale, around a norm … in relation to one another'

(Foucault 1977, p. 223), and ranked accordingly as 'job ready', 'hard to reach' or 'pre-NEET' (LSN 2009; Bainbridge and Browne 2010; Gracey and Kelly 2010; Lee and Wright 2011). Therefore the NEET category is the latest in a long line of classifications used to position young people from stigmatised communities at the margins of society. It is a disciplinary technique that enables the myriad private institutions that provide job search services to pin down the activities of the urban poor. This process is underpinned by a very narrow debate regarding gang-related and knife crime among inner-city youth that ignores the complex layers of activity of young people in these geographical locations. Yet within proximate view, these maligned urban environments are a locus for an abundance of entrepreneurial activity and spirit.

I have used grime music as a way to articulate and bring to the fore the education, employment and training that people in the NEET category are engaged in. In his *Rebel with a Cause* album intro, veteran MC Ghetts details his longevity in the grime music scene and charts his journey from 'being kicked out of school' and becoming NEET, to ending up in Feltham, a young offenders institution (Ghetts 2014). That might have been the end of his story – remaining out of sight or unable to locate (UTL). Instead, he continues to have a highly visible and influential presence as an independent recording artist, creating music, selling it online and performing live. I have shown that young people like Ghetts, often classified as NEET, mature and evolve through participation in the urban music sector. At the same time as offering a mechanism for reinvention and exit, participation in this economy throws up a whole host of negative stereotypes. Nevertheless it is evident that for the practitioners there are distinct possibilities that are enabled by their musical practice. The urban music economy is a complex fabric of ethnically stigmatised groups and the white working class, and it affords opportunities for employment in a diminishing labour market.

The NEET category disguises and obscures the enterprising activities of young people from poor areas. Funding and policy strategies such as Jobseekers Allowance (GOV.UK 2014) and the National Apprenticeship Programme (Mirza-Davies 2014) presume that those who are deemed to be NEET are doing nothing at all. The reduction of youth unemployment levels constitutes a major challenge for governments across the globe, and entrepreneurship may be a crucial way to increase employment and stimulate job creation (Schoof 2006). Entrepreneurs have a distinctive presence; what they do in general and who they are as individuals create images of an entrepreneurial identity (Anderson and Warren 2011). By foregrounding the entrepreneurial activities of participants in the urban music economy, I have shown that the existing definitions of who is an entrepreneur and what constitutes enterprise and entrepreneurship are key questions that require further examination. However, the processes by which these practitioners acquire the knowledge required for business planning, marketing and promotion as well as sales and financial skills require further research. Through the creation of business and self-employment, young people can navigate a course to economic independence at a time when traditional labour markets are shrinking.

Why grime music matters

Grime music is something of a puzzle: it is hyperlocalised, by which I mean it specifically relates to place, and it is possible to hear the communities that make up east London past and present. In Chapter 2, I traced the genealogy of this music genre back to the Jamaican sound systems and their UK counterparts. Grime is a sonic representation of its origins – the council estates and street corners of inner-city east London – but it reaches back into, and is nourished by, black diaspora connections. When DJ Kool Herc brought hip-hop to the Bronx, he was reinterpreting a music genre from his childhood in Jamaica, which had its roots/routes in North American R n B (Chang 2007). The post-World War II migrants from the Jamaican countryside adapted the sound system format for the enclosed spaces of England. By the start of the twenty-first century, grime artists such as Wiley and Kano had extended the creative practice of the Jamaican sound system and its constituent sound clash by rhyming or 'spitting' over disrupted, disjointed beats. Grime draws on the cultural, political and economic history of having parents and grandparents from elsewhere and on the cultural intermixture that takes place between black and white working-class youth on street corners and housing estates. It is this social and cultural flow through inner-city east London from which grime emerged and took its place on a global stage.

On the face of it, there is no immediate link between *Pow!*, the iconic 2008 grime music anthem, and a BAFTA award-winning English actress. Yet this connection between Maxwell Ansah, aka grime MC Lethal Bizzle, and Dame Judi Dench highlights the complex ecology of entrepreneurship in the UK's urban music economy. We are told – over and over – that young people in these areas operate in postcode silos. This may be true on some levels. But with and through music, young people operate collaboratively to produce and disseminate their musical practice.

Narratives of resistance and resilience

I have documented and analysed what the participants in the urban music economy are doing and I have also considered how they create meaning from what they do. I wanted to give an account that is not preoccupied with the illicit – that is, unregistered – activities of those participating in the urban music economy. Therefore, I have aimed for a narrative that explores entrepreneurship in its broadest sense and foregrounds the participants' understanding and control of their cultural practice. In Chapter 3 I put forward the concept of the artist-entrepreneur and illustrated the inputs and influences that impact on my informants in the sector.

Through enterprise and enterprising activities in the urban music economy young black men, including those who are categorised as NEET – marginalisation notwithstanding – are drawing on a continuity of practice to create meaningful work for themselves and others, And having something to do is key, because if one is doing something, then it opens up the possibility of being something. As Fred opines at the start of the chapter, participation allows young people to keep out of trouble. But it is much more than that: these participants have used urban music to articulate the nature of their living conditions, to speak of the lack of opportunity and to create a route to employment in the creative and cultural industries, sectors that continue to be an exclusively white and middle-class enclave. Through serving apprenticeships with sound systems and grime crews, by watching and working with others, these practitioners have used their creativity to establish ways to earn a living. This is detailed in Chapters 3 and 4.

From my research, carried out in east London and Cyprus, I have shown that entrepreneurship in the urban music economy may provide self-employment, new jobs, business start-up and economic movement for young people. This micro-entrepreneurship can offer a bottom-up method for generating an income, self-reliance and an innovative path to earning a living. In the case study from Ayia Napa in Chapter 5, I show that far from being a highly localised niche activity, as is often assumed, the unlikely juxtaposition of barbershops and curry goat in Cyprus illustrates how young people from impoverished backgrounds use music to create work and generate wealth in an international arena.

Independent artists in the grime music scene have used advances in technology to establish national and global audiences for their creative output, in near and distant locations. Technology has allowed them to transcend distance and connect with a wider constituency without the need for intermediaries. Within the urban music economy, grime can therefore travel unaccompanied by the participants. The practitioners can go or not go to where their creative expression is being heard.

I now turn to the key contradictions and questions that arise from my exploration of the urban music economy. It is clear that in these dense urban settings notions of nation remain in the background when people come together to make music, whatever their cultural heritage. However, this conviviality is contingent on an ongoing process of negotiation. This cultural intermezzo also raises questions regarding who belongs to and who can speak for 'the ends', or the local neighbourhood (Back 1996, p. 240). The question of who can claim ownership of this practice and who can speak of, and for, the neighbourhood is highly nuanced. This is particularly germane if certain genres of music, like grime, have been used to articulate the lived experiences of those who occupy a specific, physical place.

It is also evident that to cross borders into new identities as artist-entrepreneurs, commerce and creativity must combine; therefore the consequences of 'being a brand' need to be further explored and examined. Furthermore, a more complex reading of the urban music sector reveals a creative practice that mimics neo-liberalist endeavours, in that it is highly individualised yet adopts a collaborative, partnership approach.

Those that participate in the urban music economy building creative enterprises construct a model of entrepreneurship where the artist is the brand. Yet the demand from consumers for more and more creative output, coupled with the unwillingness to pay for music, means that in many respects urban music artists may face a precarious existence. Furthermore, in a neo-liberal framework success or failure begins and ends with you. If all is attributed to personal responsibility, what happens if your dream 'fails'? How is it possible to manage the existential crisis when your dream is no more or is radically altered?

I have looked at constructions of entrepreneurship in a sector that traditionally has had little attention from the academy. This book opens up a dialogue with the participants in this economy and relays what they are doing in their own words and actions. The artist-entrepreneurs who are the core informants for this book are working for love and money. Yet because their activities do not conform to existing tropes of inertia and lack of aspiration among the urban poor, they remain invisible to policymakers. As an artistic product, the cultural value of the music they produce is negligible until there is a possibility for profit by the mainstream (Khomami 2016). During a five-year period, I encountered young men and women who have used their creative practice to uncover a different way of being in the world. In so doing, movement and transformation become real prospects, despite the material constraints of 'the ends'.

I have used ethnographic evidence gleaned from interviews and observations to offer an interpretation, rather than an explanation, of the rhythms of the urban music economy in east London and beyond. I have become attuned to the story of what it means to be an artist-entrepreneur in 'the ends'. I have also looked carefully at how musical creative practice emerges from these inner east London boroughs and is then widely disseminated throughout the UK and abroad. I am aware that I am speaking in the place of others, so I have aimed to present the participants/informants as the rounded, three-dimensional individuals who met with me, spoke to me and gave their time because they wanted their story to be told in an academic arena, 'on a serious level' (from field notes).

I have endeavoured to engage with this world in a different way, by going on a journey. This journey has captured the sounds and vibrations of this environment – urban east London –to provide a frame of reference with which to understand how it is that grime music emerged from this location. Just as important is how grime has broken free of its east London origins. Grime, and the wider urban music sector have a social, economic and cultural impact that cannot and should not be underestimated.

Note

1 After housing costs have been taken in to account.

References

Anderson, A.R. and Warren, L., 2011. The entrepreneur as hero and jester: Enacting the entrepreneurial discourse. *International Small Business Journal*, 29(6), pp. 589–609.

Back, L., 1996. *New ethnicities and urban culture*, UCL Press. Available at: https://books.google.co.uk/books/about/New_Ethnicities_and_Urban_Culture.html?id=m W906f1B9zkC [accessed 14 January 2016].

Bainbridge, L. and Browne, A., 2010. *Generation Neet*, York: Report for Children and Young People Now Magazine.

BBC News Channel, 2003. Rapper Rascal wins Mercury Prize. *BBC*. Available at: http://news.bbc.co.uk/1/hi/entertainment/music/3092520.stm [accessed 11 September 2010].

Chang, J., 2007. *Can't stop won't stop: a history of the hip-hop generation*, London: Ebury.

Children's Commissioner, 2013. They go the extra mile: Reducing inequality in school exclusions, London, UK: HMSO.

Communities and Local Government, 2007. REACH Report. Available at: www.communities.gov.uk/publications/communities/reachreport [accessed 15 September, 2010].

Department for Children, Schools and Families, 2010. *A guide to enterprise education: For enterprise coordinators, teachers and leaders at schools*, London, UK: HMSO.

Directgov, 2011. [ARCHIVED CONTENT]. Available at: http://webarchive.national archives.gov.uk/+/www.direct.gov.uk/en/Employment/Jobseekers/LookingForWork/DG_184167 [accessed 24 May 2014].

du Bois-Reymond, M., 2004. Youth, Learning, Europe: Ménage à Trois? *Young* 12(3), pp. 187–204.

Foucault, M., 1977. *Discipline and punish: The birth of the prison*. Harmondsworth: Penguin.

Ghetts, 2014. *Rebel with a cause*, London, UK: Disrupt Ltd.

GOV.UK, 2014. Jobseeker's Allowance (JSA). Available at: www.gov.uk/jobseekers-allowance [accessed 14 May 2014].

Grabiner, A.S., 2000. The informal economy: A report, London, UK: HMSO.

Gracey, S. and Kelly, S., 2010. *Changing the NEET mindset: Achieving more effective transitions between education and work*, London, UK: LSN.

Hanna, K. & Bosetti, N., 2015. *Inside out: The new geography of wealth and poverty in London*, London, UK: Centre for London.

HM Government, 2007. Index of multiple deprivation (IMD) 2007/Neighbourhood statistics data. Dataset resource DGU. Available at: http://data.gov.uk/dataset/index_of_multiple_deprivation_imd_2007/resource/48aa7db3-b932-4d64-bec8-f63bd3290d91 [accessed 27 July 2013].

Khomami, N., 2016. BBC Radio 1 music boss: Grime will be Britain's next big cultural export. *Guardian*. Available at: www.theguardian.com/uk-news/2016/mar/12/bbc-radio-1-music-boss-grime-britain-chris-price-1xtra [accessed 18 March 2016].

Lee, N. and Wright, J., 2011. *Off the map? The geography of NEETs: A snapshot analysis for the Private Equity Foundation*, Lancaster University: Work Foundation.

LSN, 2009. *Tackling the NEETs problem*, London: LSN.

Mirza-Davies, 2014. *Apprenticeships policy*, House of Commons Library.

Ofsted, 2011. *Economics, business and enterprise education*, Manchester, UK: Ofsted.

Prince's Trust Enterprise Programme, 2014. The Prince's Trust Enterprise programme: Setting young people up business, support for small businesses. Available at: www.princes-trust.org.uk/need_help/enterprise_programme.aspx [accessed 24 May 2014].

Schoof, U., 2006. *Stimulating youth entrepreneurship: Barriers and incentives to enterprise start-ups by young people*, Geneva: International Labour Office.

Sergeant, H., 2009. *Wasted: The betrayal of white working class and black Caribbean boys*, London: Centre for Policy Studies.

Sparkes, J., 1999. Schools, education and social exclusion, London, UK: Centre for Analysis of Social Exclusion.

Start Up Loans, 2013. About Us. Available at: www.startuploans.co.uk/about-us/ [accessed 24 May 2014].

UK Parliament, 2012. Youth unemployment and the Youth Contract. *UK Parliament.* Available at: www.parliament.uk/business/committees/committees-a-z/commons-select/ work-and-pensions-committee/inquiries/youth-unemployment-and-the-future-jobs-fund/ [accessed 24 May 2014]

Wicks, S., 2013. Should enterprise education be introduced to the national curriculum? Available at: www.enterprisenation.com/blog/should-enterprise-education-be-introduced-to-the-national-curriculum/ [accessed 13 July 2013].

Williams, C.C. and Nadin, S., 2012. Work beyond employment: Representations of informal economic activities. *Work, Employment & Society* 26(2), pp. 1–10.

Appendix 1
The research sample

Background to the research question

I am a black woman of Caribbean heritage. I was born in England to parents who migrated from Jamaica in the 1950s. Within this context, I grew up with reggae music and sound systems. I experienced the blues dance as a cultural and creative activity, but also as an enterprise. The music, however, was key: it was what drew the crowd to an event. When I started out on this research project I was in my mid-forties. Music had been an integral part of negotiating my identity, particularly at a time when being black and being English were mutually exclusive categories. The *Mighty Diamonds – Right Time* album was a defining moment because it talked of Africa as 'home', when my Jamaican heritage and English location had told me that 'home' was always elsewhere. *Burning Spear* gave a new reading of Jamaican history by insisting that 'Christopher Columbus was a damned blasted liar'.

I was born in Brixton and grew up in a pre-gentrified Hammersmith in West London. However, for the last forty years, I have lived in the London borough of Newham. I have watched this area change as it emerged from an area that scored low on most economic and social indicators into one of the host boroughs for the London 2012 Olympics. And yet the three most deprived boroughs in London continue to be Hackney, Tower Hamlets and Newham – in that order (HM Government 2007).

In 1978 I began my first 'official' job, working at the London International Freight Terminal (LIFT) deep in the industrial heartland of Stratford. LIFT was on the site of what is now the Queen Elizabeth Olympic Park (Royal Geographical Society 2009). Since then, my occupational background has been primarily within the education and training sector. Some years ago, I qualified as a teacher and taught adults of all ages in a number of settings. Furthermore, my route to higher education was far from traditional: I left school at the age of 16 with a handful of O levels and worked in a sausage factory in the London borough of Hackney. My subsequent working life in the public sector has been underpinned by part-time study as a mature student. However, it was my work as a lecturer in the further education sector that brought me into contact with the most challenging young people – disengaged is perhaps too mild a word to describe those who were reluctant students in colleges in east, north and south London. These students had been schooled in the midst of the various education policy changes so aptly described by Tomlinson (Tomlinson 2005). So when I was asked by the London borough of Newham to take students on for work experience, I was keen to do so.

When I started this project, I was a successful business owner, an entrepreneur. After two decades as an employee, I craved the autonomy and the independence that self-employment brings. Over time, however, I identified and exploited various gaps in the market in my particular industry. As a consequence, my business grew, I employed staff and I branched out into areas related to education and training. I created a nimble, flexible business that was responsive to customer need, and I was proud of this.

When I started my business in 2004, I was based in Silvertown and although I had lived in the London borough of Newham for a long time, I had visited this area only once before. Silvertown and Canning Town are areas in the south of the borough that had a significant far right (National Front) presence in the late 1970s, effectively creating no go areas for ethnic minority communities (Correa 2005). In those days, black and white people operated and socialised in very separate spheres; it was a very polarised existence. Now, there is a certain hard-fought, albeit partial, conviviality – and a new East End is in evidence (Gilroy 2004a). And while it is beyond the scope of this project to analyse these changes, it assists in laying the ground for the context of my research.

This research project, therefore, came out of all of my areas of interest: enterprise, education and young people – especially those deemed to be NEET. At the outset, I did not know what to expect. I had a notion that although secondary schools in England have been non-selective since the 1970s, young people from poor backgrounds on the whole did less well in terms of educational achievement. In addition, the REACH project concluded that black boys and young black men face serious challenges in every sector of society. They are less likely to do well at school, more likely to be unemployed and much more likely to become involved in the criminal justice system (Communities and Local Government 2009a, p. 6). Yet it appeared that there was a creative underground – a growing informal business sector – providing a wide range of innovative artistic and cultural services and products, and I wondered if there was any connection between the two.

I therefore had an initial hypothesis that, on the whole, those who operate within what I was then calling the creative underground had few qualifications and that their experience of formal schooling discouraged innovation, creativity and enterprise because of the need to meet national government targets and outcomes.

My project therefore considered how this creative economy was constituted and what entrepreneurial activities the practitioners within this arena undertake. I focused on music as a creative sector because this seemed to be a common thread among the young people I met as they came into my place of business. These young people appeared to be both producers and consumers of music, and it therefore gave me a way in. By learning about the relevant music genres, I was able to explore, understand and begin to articulate the wider networks and inter-connections of the informal creative economy as it relates to east London.

Before I was in a position to ask any questions, though, I had to get a feel for what these young people were listening to – and sometimes creating. In so doing, my then 46-year-old ears moved rapidly from a position of 'what's that noise?' to an appreciation of the complexity of what had been created. The skill and confidence required to perform, the effort it took to learn your craft, all became apparent in the months I spent watching Channel U, Channel AKA and YouTube and listening to a multiplicity of pirate and internet radio stations.

The attainment of five GCSEs grade A*–C constituted a golden ticket, in that it afforded entrance to the more highly regarded further education courses such as A levels. However, although the majority of my informants had not achieved this level of qualification and were therefore excluded from the field of further and higher education, they were in fact highly competent creative practitioners.

Also, I discovered that many of these young people, who would ordinarily be classified as NEET, were in fact establishing and developing microbusinesses in the urban music economy. They were selling mixtapes of their own work, for example, or providing film and video services. It also became apparent that some of this business activity had a reach beyond the local area. As I met with and spoke to my informants, my increasing knowledge of the logic and practice of their creative output gave me a certain credibility, particularly as I was outside of the usual demographic for a grime music fan. It demonstrated my real interest in what they were doing and how they were doing it. There was a recognition that I was not approaching them or their work with the usual stereotypical short-hand relating to guns, gangs and drugs.

In time, I could make connections with my own musical tastes and business experience and practice, which at first had seemed far removed. I still maintain a deep respect and admiration for the work the participants in this sector undertake. Artists learn their craft and use their passion for what they do to create self-employment and work opportunities for others. Those that were able to do this created sustainable businesses and an opportunity for a line of flight from very impoverished circumstances.

Another aspect that I unearthed, fairly early on, was that far from being underground the urban music economy is very much on the ground and highly visible. The participants in this sector were early adopters of technology and social media, which enabled a democratic distribution of creative practice. The prolific use of technology – for example, links to music on Twitter or posting videos on YouTube – to promote creative practice was a revelation. The 'informal economy' that it had been assumed these participants operated in was in fact positioned and anchored in the formal economy, and there was no clear distinction between the two sectors.

I conducted my field research by using a combination of semi-structured interviews comprising a small number of core questions and participant observation in nightclubs, cultural seminars, video shoots, fashion shoots and pirate radio stations. I selected East London as a location because, for me, it is a familiar setting having lived and worked in the area for more than thirty years. For the purposes of this research, east London is defined as the London boroughs of Newham, Tower Hamlets, Hackney and Waltham Forest.

In total, I carried out forty semi-structured interviews over a five-year period, from October 2007 to November 2012. The interviews took place in two locations, London and Ayia Napa, Cyprus. In the UK, I interviewed twenty-three participants in the urban music economy. In Cyprus, I spoke with artists/performers, holidaymakers and one business owner. The majority of the respondents were participants in the urban music economy.

My research sample is therefore representative of the most common roles and activities within the sector: DJs from pirate, licensed and internet radio, MCs, event promoters, models, model agency owners, music producers and managing directors of online TV channels.

For the purpose of reporting the research findings, I have changed all respondents' names to provide anonymity. However, because the informants' creative output is in the public domain, some identifying features might still be evident.

How I obtained the study sample

My occupational background is as a teacher and trainer in the further education sector and within this context I often met young people who were disengaged from, and disillusioned by, formal education. Also, as a business owner I had taken on a number of school students aged fifteen and sixteen on work experience. I had also been invited to participate in Enterprise Week at various secondary schools in the London borough of Newham. Enterprise Week consisted of a variety of activities for fifteen- and sixteen-year-olds to enable them to experience a taste of the business world. Enterprise Week – now known as Global Entrepreneurship Week – is a national government initiative set up to encourage young people to be more enterprising because enterprise and entrepreneurship are seen as key to economic success.

On the whole, the majority of students placed with us had been deemed by their schools to be difficult to manage or low achievers and therefore at risk of becoming NEET. Andrew, who later became one of my key informants, was one of those students placed with us who, according to his head of year, was at risk of becoming NEET. Most of these young people, whatever their ethnic or cultural backgrounds, were interested in music – listening to it, sharing it or watching it on MySpace. Indeed, most were more likely to have headphones than a pen while on work placement.

Further discussions with Andrew, one of my key informants, allowed me to identify this popular genre as grime. Once I had the name of the sound, I could view it on Channel U and YouTube and listen to it on pirate radio stations. After several months of careful listening, I was then able to map current key practitioners and locate grime in its geographical and historical context.

To find respondents, I used a snowball sampling method and was also guided by my key informants, who made suggestions about who else to interview. For example, Andrew suggested that I contact James (formerly a grime DJ, then a funky house DJ), and James put me in touch with Ian (a DJ). Fred introduced me to Brian (a reggae DJ whose father was one of the 1970s sound system pioneers).

I also used word of mouth and chance encounters. For example, once word got out that I was 'writing a book about grime', people self-selected and started to contact me directly. This is how I met George (a music producer), one of only four respondents who had gone on to higher education, and Helen – a singer-songwriter, with a stage school background. Sam had come to my office to meet up with a friend of his who was working with us as a graphic designer. Sam was a former MC who had become a film-maker – his films and videos have appeared on Channel AKA and YouTube and featured some of the artists who I had already interviewed.

I also used a direct approach: requesting for interview via email, which had some limited success. These contact details were widely available through social media sites such as Facebook, Twitter and YouTube. Fiona, a 24-year-old music video director, was one of the interviews that came about this way. She had created videos for a number of the artists on Channel AKA and had shot videos for some of my informants.

I met her on set at a digital TV station in Hoxton, where she was filming a music video. While I was there, her video overran because the lead artist had been held up. During this time Fiona introduced me to her make-up artist, who agreed to an interview. At that shoot, I interviewed five people in total because the opportunity presented itself while I watched and waited for several hours. These chance encounters offered not only the opportunity of an interview but also a discreet method to capture the experience of being behind the scenes.

In terms of informants, by mid 2011, my sample still contained no female performers, so I emailed a female MC, Mary. (I also emailed two other female MCs but had no response.) Mary was an independent MC who had recently made a comeback after a quiet period in terms of her creative output. She agreed to an interview, seeming very keen at first, but she then referred me to her agent, who then gave me the brush-off. This process went back and forth for several months. Locations and venues were identified and agreed then changed or cancelled at the last minute. Finally, Mary had tour dates in Europe and there came a point when persistence was futile, so I gave up on her. In 2012, while reviewing the transcripts from the field research, I realised that I had a gap in terms of respondents from the online television channel sector. I therefore sent an email request to one of these channels and Steven kindly responded and offered his time. The final interview was with him, the managing director of a TV channel that had broadcast the creative output from the majority of my research informants.

1 Interviews

Table A1.1 Interviews

LONDON

1	ANDREW	RECORDING ARTIST/MC	18
2	BRIAN	DJ	40
3	CHARLOTTE	MODEL	18
4	DIANE	BUSINESS OWNER/MODEL	29
5	EDWARD	MC	20
6	FRED	DJ/EVENT PROMOTER	40
7	GEORGE	PRODUCER	24
8	HELEN	SINGER/SONGWRITER	18
9	IAN	DJ/CLUB & RADIO	22
10	JAMES	DJ/ONLINE RADIO	25
11	SAM	FILM/VIDEO MAKER	24
12	ADAM	MC	18
13	BERNARD	MC	18
14	VICTOR*	DJ	33
15	QUENTIN*	VOCALIST/HOST	34
16	COLIN	PRODUCER	24
17	DAVID	MC/BUSINESS OWNER	26
18	ERIC	DJ/NATIONAL RADIO	
19	FIONA	MUSIC VIDEO DIRECTOR/FILM MAKER	24
20	GILLIAN	MAKE UP ARTIST/STYLIST	27
21	HARVEY	MC/BUSINESS OWNER	28
22	JOHN	RECORDING ARTIST/MC	
23	STEVEN	MANAGING DIRECTOR/ONLINE TV CHANNEL	25

AYIA NAPA

24	KEVIN	DJ/MC/EVENT PROMOTER	30
25	LIONEL	ENTREPRENEUR	32
26	MICHAEL	DJ	28
	QUENTIN*	VOCALIST/HOST	33
27	PETER	DJ	34
28	OLIVER	MC/PRODUCER	30
29	RICHARD	MC	18
30	WILLIAM	PRODUCER	19
	VICTOR*	DJ	31
31	NEVILLE	EVENT PROMOTER	31
32	XAVIER	EVENT PROMOTER	31
33	TYRONE	MC	18
34	ARNOLD	MC/VOCALIST	

HOLIDAYMAKERS – AYIA NAPA

35	NATALIE
36	GEORGIA
37	JESSICA
38	LAUREN
39	SHANICE
40	TOM

---

* interviewed twice

Research participants: summary analysis of data

Table A1.2 Age at time of interview (*N* = 40)

AGE	
18	6
19–21	2
22–24	5
25–27	4
28–30	4
31–33	5
34–36	1
37–40	2
NOT SPECIFIED	

Table A1.3 Ethnicity

ETHNICITY		
WEST AFRICAN	5	NIGERIA, GHANA
EAST AFRICAN	1	UGANDA
CARIBBEAN	19	
ENGLISH	7	
GREEK – CYPRIOT	1	
INDIAN	1	
MIXED PARENTAGE	1	ENGLISH/NIGERIAN
NOT SPECIFIED	5	

Table A1.4 Gender

GENDER	
MALE	30
FEMALE	10 (five practitioners in the urban music economy and five holidaymakers in Ayia Napa)

Table A1.5 Geographical location

GEOGRAPHICAL LOCATION (of the informant)	
LONDON	Plaistow, Walthamstow, Hackney, Forest Gate, Manor Park, Tottenham, Custom House, Beckton, Chiswick, Redhill, New Cross
OUTSIDE LONDON	Manchester, Wolverhampton, Birmingham, Reading, Gloucester

Table A1.6 Qualifications

QUALIFICATIONS	
MASTERS DEGREE	1
DEGREE	4 (including informant with Masters Degree)
A LEVELS	4 (including informants with Degree and Masters Degree)
5 GCSE A* – C	5
LESS THAN 5 GCSE A* – C	6
NONE	6
NOT SPECIFIED	14

Table A1.7 Age left full time education

AGE LEFT FULL TIME EDUCATION	
BELOW 16	2
16	10
17	3
18	4
OVER 18	4
NOT SPECIFIED	17

References

Communities and Local Government, 2009. An experimental test of the impact of Black role model messages: Technical report. Available at: http://communities.gov.uk/publications/communities/reachmessagestechnical [accessed 15 September 2010].

Correa, R., 2005. Investigating links between racial harassment and (un)employment and employability in the black and minority ethnic communities of the London Borough of Newham. London: Community Links.

Gilroy, P., 2004. *After empire: Melancholia or convivial culture?* London, UK: Routledge.

HM Government, 2007. Index of Multiple Deprivation (IMD) 2007. Available at: http://data.gov.uk/dataset/index_of_multiple_deprivation_imd_2007/resource/48aa7db3-b932-4d64-bec8-f63bd3290d91 [accessed 27 July 2013].

Royal Geographical Society, 2009. Stratford. Available at: www.rgs.org/OurWork/Schools/Fieldwork+and+local+learning/Planning+your+fieldtrip/Fieldwork+locations/London+2012+Olympic+Park/Stratford.htm [accessed 27 July 2013].

Tomlinson, S., 2005. *Education in a post-welfare society*, 2nd edn, Maidenhead, UK: Open University Press.

Appendix 2

Reflections on method

My research question was primarily concerned with the experience of being in and participating in a particular social world, namely the informal urban music economy. I had initially wanted to explore the learning choices and educational achievements of participants within this sector and I had posited a link between being NEET, educational underachievement and participation in the informal economy.

My starting point was the constant music soundtrack that accompanied life in east London in 2007, whether broadcast from mobile phones or brought in to my office with the young people who undertook work experience at my place of business. These fifteen- and sixteen-year-olds had on the whole been categorised as at risk of being NEET. The underpinning refrain of this time was the 'post-code war', guns, gangs and knives and the general terror of the hooded monster, menacing and desensitised to everyday human suffering (De Castella 2007; Glendinning 2008). In 2008, fifty-five young men were stabbed to death in the UK. Explicit links were made in the media to suggest a connection between the escalating violence and gang membership to grime music (Barnett 2006; Rose 2008).

I therefore wanted to undertake a scholarly inquiry into the notion of the informal creative economy as it related to grime music. Focusing on sixteen to forty-year-olds in east London, my research project had three key objectives: first, to identify existing formal qualifications; second, to explore the learning choices of those within the sector and the learning opportunities within the hidden or underground creative economy; and finally, to identify ways to harness the skills, talents and energy of these participants and translate that into formal qualifications and legitimate business pursuits.

My research question therefore lent itself to an ethnographic approach as it is primarily concerned with the experience of being in and participating in a particular social world – in this case the informal urban music economy. Ethnography involves being with, observing and taking part during ordinary activities over a period of time to write an account of selected aspects of life as it is experienced in that world (Emerson *et al.* 1995; Van Maanen 2011).

The ethnographic context

A key focus of my research project is the enterprising activities of participants in the informal urban music economy who may be classified as NEET. I therefore adopted a classic ethnographic approach to establish a rapport, select informants and transcribe interviews. Nevertheless, Geertz suggests this is not the key purpose of the undertaking and what the ethnographer is actually trying to do is pick their way through structures of 'inference and implication' and bring forth a thick description of the culture being studied (Geertz 1973, p. 7). That said, the task of the ethnographer is to find a way to grasp the complex conceptual structures of the object of study and relay them back to the outside world (Geertz 1973, p. 10). I have therefore designed this project so that it is possible to observe, examine and analyse the complex structures of the informal creative economy as it pertains to urban music.

My research constitutes an attempt, albeit on a small scale, to discover not only what the participants in this social world are doing, but also how they create meaning from what they do. I have aimed for a narrative that explores the nature of enterprise in the urban music economy and foregrounds the participants' understanding and control of their cultural practice. Although Geertz suggests cultural research is a search for, or an analysis of, meaning rather than a quest to establish laws and rules (Geertz 1973), I began this project wanting to describe the urban music economy from an insider perspective and to provide a dense and textured description of this world (Koro-Ljungberg and Greckhamer 2005). I also want to identify the logic and practice of this economy.

The US ghetto of East Harlem in the late 1980s and early 1990s is perhaps far removed from the inner-city area of east London that was my geographical starting point in 2007. The sustained observation that Bourgois undertook was at a time prior to and during the crack cocaine epidemic. As he lived with his family in East Harlem, this was his neighbourhood and the people he studied were his neighbours, Bourgois was therefore able to conduct his observation over a period of many years (Bourgois 2003). He wanted to show normal people carrying out their everyday activities and seeking social meaning and respect in an environment of poverty. For Bourgois, an ethnographic approach allowed him to look beyond the usual focus on visible self-destructive outcomes of living in impoverished environments – such as street drug dealing and illegal drug consumption. Instead, he was able to consider structural forces that propel people to do what they do on the streets: poor schools and little access to jobs. My resources did not allow for the same level of observation over an elongated time period, but I live and work in the same location as my initial respondents. I was therefore able to observe the field of study over a period of time.

I also wanted to give an account that is not preoccupied with the illicit – that is, unregistered – activities of those participating in the urban music economy. Therefore, I have aimed for a narrative that explores entrepreneurship in its broadest sense and foregrounds the participants' understanding and control of their cultural practice (Jansson 2013, p. 137). My aim is to present the participants/informants as the rounded, three-dimensional individuals who met with me, spoke to me and gave their time because they wanted their story to be told in an academic arena. My participation in the field of enquiry is made transparent and explicit.

Drawing on various concepts of the role of the ethnographer, Atkinson suggests that the aim of the ethnographer is to 'make the familiar strange and the strange familiar' (Atkinson *et al.* 2003, p. 17). My research was to take place on familiar ground – urban east London – but in a social world unfamiliar to me. The ethnographic approach adopted by Hesmondhalgh and Baker in *A Very Complicated Version of Freedom* to examine the experience of workers in the cultural industries is relevant here (Hesmondhalgh and Baker 2011a). Their aim was to build on recent studies of working conditions, which looked at the political and economic dynamics and organisational structure of the creative sector, and to address the gaps in research on the qualitative aspects of working in this sector. Drawing on the 'logics' used by Miége to model the structure of different types of cultural production, they cultivated a sample of respondents carrying out particular types of cultural work. The three models, or 'logics', they made use of were publishing, flow and written press. The interviewees were gleaned from a range of genres within these models (in music, hip-hop and electronic dance music; in flow, television; and in written press, magazines). In addition, certain characteristics that represent the spread of the sector were also accounted for in their sample, such as freelance and salaried workers, corporate and independent practitioners and aspiring and established individuals. As well as the interviews, they carried out ethnographic fieldwork in a London-based independent television production company (Hesmondhalgh and Baker 2011b).

The research sample for participants in my project is therefore representative of the most common roles and activities within the sector. I interviewed forty people involved in the urban music economy, the majority of whom had key roles in the sector. I also undertook participant observation in locations where this creative practice was carried out, for example backstage at music video shoots and on location at pirate radio station broadcasts. The sample includes DJs from pirate, licensed and internet radio, MCs, event promoters, models, a model agency owner, music producers, vocalists, sound engineers, beatmakers and the managing director of an online TV channel. There is representation from the 'old hands' – those who had been in the sector for a number of years – some of whom had achieved a level of success and recognition, others of whom had adopted different guises or new pursuits or both. Aspiring and established independent artists are also represented in the study.

The combination of interview – and the fieldwork they undertook in a television company – enabled Hesmondhalgh and Baker to highlight the contradictions and tensions in their field of enquiry. The political and structural forces that shape the creative sector are also explored through the ethnographic method (Hesmondhalgh and Baker 2011b).

Paul Willis's influential research undertaken in a secondary modern school in the West Midlands used an ethnographic approach to uncover and analyse the methods by which non-academic white working-class boys become who they are supposed to be – 'lads' destined for manual labour and factory work (Willis 1993). Willis drew his sample from a school population of 600, and although the school contained 'substantial West Indian and Asian minorities', their experiences were excluded 'for the sake of clarity and incision' (Willis 1993, p. 2). He looked at how twelve 'lads' created a school counterculture where life experience and practical ability had more value (because they had more use in their world) than the formal knowledge the school system was trying to impart. Although they rejected conformity and opposed authority, the counterculture that the 'lads' created actually mimicked the work environments they would inhabit after formal schooling. Through observation, discussion, case study and interview, this study foregrounded what 'the lads' thought and felt they were doing to determine their future. This study was conducted over a three-year period – 1972–1975 – that predates the rise of Thatcherism and the decline of the manufacturing sector. Since then, young people who would have gone straight into work at sixteen have been absorbed into the further education sector; those who do not inhabit the territory of either work, education or training are categorised as NEET. My research project aims to build on the work in *Learning to Labour* (Willis 1993), in that it consider the formal schooling achievements of male and female practitioners in the informal urban music economy and foregrounds the experience of those from marginalised communities.

In *Deep Play: Notes on the Balinese Cockfight* Geertz's participation in an illegal cockfight (including fleeing from the police raid) afforded him entry into a field that until then had been closed to him. His participation rather than passive observation provided an opportunity for acceptance by the members of the community. Being able to share some common ground – in the retelling of the raid – opened up a rapport with those same villagers who had previously ignored his existence (Geertz 1973). It is clear, then, that being visible does not automatically provide a way into the field: it is necessary to participate as well as observe, therefore active participation is a core component of my methodology.

Nevertheless, immersion into the field (when that field pertains to electronic dance music and festivals) is often viewed with suspicion in academic research circles (O'Grady 2013, p. 1). A horizontal research method, where the researcher is 'situated alongside colleagues, participants, and audience members acknowledging that they are part of the transaction that is under investigation' and working to understand that creative practice from within, can be useful in this context (O'Grady 2013, p. 20). This horizontal research method is germane because in this object of study, creative practice is carried out in nightclubs, in radio stations and on filmsets. This type of practice research tends to be more collaborative as it engages with ideas of space, identity and spectatorship; indeed, the relationship between the researched and the researcher is flexible and fluid (O'Grady 2013). However, it is not without its difficulties: as a researcher, I can never be fully immersed in the activity – there has to be, because of the nature of the task at hand, some caution (explicit or implicit), to be able to capture what is being experienced. Also, festivals and nightclubs are dynamic and chaotic places, and it is difficult to interrupt play with cameras, question-naires and voice recorders (O'Grady 2013, p. 35).

As a researcher, I am poised between intimacy and distance; I have to get close enough to see what is going on. I wanted to explore how the imposed experience of being an urban black male with its focus on, for example, being NEET, underachievement at school, contact with the criminal justice system and lack of employment opportunities contrasts with the chosen experience of being artists and entrepreneurs (Pickering 2008, p. 19). I wanted to find out to what extent, if any, this imposed experience contributed to propelling young people to participate in the informal creative economy.

An ethnographic approach was more likely to make the realities of this field of study visible because by 'being there' I would be able to see for myself and have an opportunity to 'draw up an approximation of the experience' (Emerson *et al.* 1995, p. 28), albeit with the caveat that experience cannot just be reported 'as it happens' – it needs to be explored and interpreted (Pickering 2008, p. 19). This experience can be near or distant, but it is not possible to be inside anoth-er's experience. Rather, the task of the researcher is to analyse and identify what the participants think that they are doing and describe events that are of social significance in that world.

For Katz, the position of the ethnographer involves 'moving between the gods and the mortals' – that is, operating out in the field, observing, making notes and relationships – to report back from a near distance to those who are even further away from the object of study (Katz 2012, p. 259). It is crucial, however, to look at the creative expression within the context of the social relations of production and consumption (Willis 2006, p. 570). An ethnographic approach allows for this. Therefore, my research project is designed so that it is possible to examine the behaviour that takes place within this specific social situation, and nudge open a partially closed door pertaining to how the enterprising and performing behaviour and activities of these participants is moulded by their social and eco-nomic circumstance (Drakopoulou Dodd and Anderson 2007; Wilson and Chaddha 2009, p. 549).

Research design

To begin immersing myself in this cultural field, I decided to use a combination of semi-structured interview – comprising a small number of core questions that all respondents were asked – and participant observation as this should allow me to explore the lived experience of participants in this sector. Using experience in this way as a methodology means that the researcher gains an understanding of what is important and significant in the participants' social world. It is a useful way to 'glean any sense of what is involved in their subjectivities, self forma-tion, life histories and participation in social and cultural identities' (Pickering 2008, p. 23). A literature review either alone or in conjunction with other research methodology would not provide this – it was evident that I needed to be in the world of the artists and practitioners; to look at their creative expression, and identify the means and media they use to produce, promote and broadcast their creative practice. It was important to talk to them about how and why they do what they do. This meant carrying out participant observation in nightclubs and at cultural seminars, video shoots, model shoots and pirate radio stations.

Research parameters and participant selection

My aim was to conduct thirty semi-structured interviews with participants in what I initially calle the 'creative underground'. These participants should represent the key roles in the urban music economy. The sample size, given the fluid nature of the sector and the resources available, seemed achievable. The research was focused on 16–18 and 18–40-year-olds within the informal creative music economy who have a link to east London either through residence or performance.

I selected East London as a location because I am familiar with the setting, having lived and worked in the area for more than thirty years. Furthermore, an exploration of what I was then calling the 'creative underground' required attendance at certain unlicensed and/or unregulated venues. It seemed therefore useful to have some first-hand understanding of the geographical, social and economic context that potential respondents were operating in. I defined East London for the purpose of my research as the London boroughs of Newham, Tower Hamlets, Hackney and Waltham Forest.

Getting started: key informants

Andrew – 18

Andrew was one of the students who had undertaken work experience with us in early 2007. Later that year, his head of year asked if we could take him on an extended work placement (one day a week for a term) because his placement with a construction firm had broken down and it was felt that without time out from school, Andrew was at risk of becoming NEET. So he came to us, initially for a term and eventually for a full academic year. During this time, Andrew revealed that he was an MC, performing as an individual and also as part of a crew. He spent some of his time with us updating his MySpace site. When I asked if I could take a look, a wide range of creative and technological skill was revealed. Throughout the next few months, Andrew and I had many conversations about his creative work, his school life and his expectations for the future. He would bring in flyers and other promotional material from events he had taken part in. If you asked Andrew a question, he would answer it. If he was asked to do something, he would do it. On the whole, he was quiet but articulate, technologically savvy, confident and willing. It was difficult to recognise the young man his head of year had described as troublesome and challenging. Indeed, on his monthly monitoring visits he always expressed surprise that Andrew was not only present but also working hard and taking part. Andrew now has a significant online presence that includes two individual YouTube videos that have over one million views and a collaboration with three artists that has two-and-a-half million views. He also has, at the time of writing, more than 50,000 followers on Twitter and he has performed at major music festivals such as Lovebox and Glastonbury. In 2010, Andrew was signed by one of the major music labels. He is now an independent recording artist and has set up a limited company to house his creative business activities.

Victor – 31

I was involved in the publication of a business magazine and in late 2006, while researching a feature on young entrepreneurs, I interviewed a DJ, Victor. At the time, Victor was at the forefront of the urban music scene and subsequently became a key informant. I interviewed him twice, once while he was working on location in Ayia Napa and the following year when he came to my office because he wanted some photos for his website. In the early days of the project, I also attended an event in Shoreditch as a participant observer where Victor was DJ'ing. Victor also has a substantial online profile, both nationally and globally, performing all over the UK, as well as in Greece, Cyprus, Switzerland and the Gambia, among others. Having started out as one of the founder members of an east London grime collective, Victor was a key player in the Ayia Napa scene. He is now a DJ on a legal radio station and is co-owner of an internet radio station and a record label. Victor has 16,000 followers on Twitter. He put me in touch with Diane, a woman who had provided models for one of the videos getting enormous airplay on what was then Channel U, *Girls Luv Nasty* (alexgowers 2006). Victor hailed from an east London borough, where he had attended several secondary schools. He would have been classified as NEET.

Diane – 29

Victor had introduced Diane to me. When we first met, she was a former model who at the time ran an events promotion and artist management company. She also provided models for a number of urban music videos. Now, she has shifted her business focus to running the model agency and putting on events that promote her agency. Diane has a lifelong interest in music and more recently has developed her career as a DJ. She writes a music page for an online magazine. This summer she is booked to appear in Italy, Ibiza and Ayia Napa. She has three thousand followers on Twitter. Diane had left school at 16 and has always been self employed – formally or informally.

Fred – 40

Some years ago, I met the Relax Sound System DJs through a business associate. One of them, Fred, was still a pirate radio DJ on a station that had been existence for a number of years but had not been broadcasting for a while. Now that the station had been relaunched, Fred had a Saturday morning show – talk and music. Fred used the show to promote his other business activities: organising cultural seminars and events. It later transpired that two of the other teachers at these seminars were also former pirate radio and club DJs. I discussed with Fred the nature of my research and that I was interested in what he did as part of his creative enterprise. Eventually, he invited me along to a forthcoming Saturday radio show. Over the next eighteen months, Fred and I got to know each other better and a mutual respect developed because we both had a background in teaching, although in Fred's terms, he did not require university approval as he already had '360 degrees of knowledge' (from field notes). Fred added me to his mailing list, so that I got a text notification if an event was being staged. Fred continues to have several performance identities: as a teacher at specific community seminars and events, as a pirate radio DJ and as a community activist campaigning for equal rights and justice. Fred has moved between informal paid and unpaid creative activity since the age of sixteen. He has rarely participated in formal paid employment.

Edward – 20

Andrew introduced me to his brother, Edward. This young man, who was eighteen when I first interviewed him, had started out as a DJ and then become an MC a few years later. He was a well-known and well-respected unsigned artist with a visible local profile. Edward was also beginning to attain a national presence. I interviewed him twice: once on tape and once on film. I have also filmed behind the scenes at one of his video shoots. Since our first meeting, Edward has released two EPs. He continues to perform in the UK and abroad and has built a strong fan base, in the Czech Republic in particular. He is known for collaborating with a number of recording artists both signed and unsigned. After I had interviewed him, Edward worked with me as a mentor on one of our London Development Agency-funded programmes targeting 16–19-year-olds who were NEET or at risk of becoming so. Edward also voiced a radio advertisement for the programme (White 2013a). He has now developed a website and a range of branded merchandise (hats, hoodies and T-shirts) sold online. Edward left school at sixteen without qualifications having attended two secondary schools and a pupil referral unit in an east London borough. Edward has been classified as NEET.

Field research in Cyprus: Ayia Napa

During the initial research it became apparent that the enterprise activity had a global reach that I had not anticipated. This led me to undertake a field trip to Ayia Napa in Cyprus. The marketing campaign in the UK for the music scene in Ayia Napa begins several months before the season begins (late June/ early July), with pre-parties, events and reunions happening all over the UK. So, armed with an HD film camera and a friend I decided to record the journey from east London to southern Cyprus, to make and experience the movement that the artists had made and to talk to people at different stages of the journey. From my initial research, it was evident that there are distinct segments to 'the vibe' – the beach, the club and the after-party – and my intention was to talk to artists and creative practitioners in each location.

The ones that got away

In 2010, new tenants moved into one of the downstairs offices in the building where I worked. I spoke to the young man, Colin, who ran the business, watched him during set-up – soundproofing the room and so on – and established that he would be running a recording studio. Over time, I outlined my research project. As a music producer, he was happy to be involved, so I interviewed him. By this time, I no longer recorded on audio because I had become aware that the minimum expected was a filmed interview, therefore I recorded this encounter on my laptop.

Colin's business operated mostly in the evening and through the night, so we did not often bump into each other during the day. One day, though, he was recording with three south London-based MCs – Krept, Konan and Cashtastic. I was able to have a brief unrecorded discussion with them about their current creative output – Krept and Konan had just uploaded their version of *Otis* by Jay Z and Kanye West and had achieved four million views in four days. I was keen to talk to them about this; however, I only had time to take some photographs and then we all had to go back to work. YouTube has now removed this video amid claims that it violated their terms and conditions of service. Also, I met Wiley – the self-styled 'Godfather of Grime' when he was on his way to a meeting with Colin – one of my informants. Unfortunately, I had no phone with me, so I could not take a photograph, and even though he initially agreed to an interview, when I went downstairs to the recording studio at the agreed time, the creative tension was heightened and overwhelming, so the interview had to be abandoned. I later learned from Colin that the track he had produced that day with Wiley involved collaboration with featured artists who had a long history of animosity.

How I conducted the study

Table A2.1 Timeline for primary research activities

December 2007–March 2008	Listening to approximately 50 of the 123 of the pirate radio stations[1]	Identifying and reading relevant publications
January 2008	First contact with Fred, DJ, event promoter and promoter of cultural seminars Attendance at cultural seminar in east London	Watching YouTube and building a database of urban music videos with an east London connection[2] Watching
February 2008	First contact with Andrew – former work experience student and MC. Meeting with Andrew's parents to obtain agreement for interview	Channel U – now Channel AKA – identifying key practitioners and
April 2008	Participant observation at cultural seminar in east London Participant observation at model shoot in east London	familiarising myself with urban music genres.
May 2008	Participant observation at nightclub in Shoreditch	
August 2008	Participant observation at Rinse FM 14th birthday celebrations – London – West End	
July 2008–July 2009	Tape recorded interviews with practitioners in the urban music economy Participant observation at pirate radio station in east London	Watching the urban chart every Saturday on Channel U. Watching
July 2009	Participant observation at a cultural seminar in South London hosted by Fred	films which had urban music as a soundtrack, for
August 2009	Participant observation and filmed interviews in Ayia Napa – Southern Cyprus	example, *Kidulthood* (*Menhaj Huda 2006*)
October 2009	Additional tape recorded interview with internet film producer	*Adulthood* (*Noel Clarke 2008*), *Life & Lyrics*,
November 2009	Filmed interview and observation at pirate radio station	(*Richard Laxton 2006*),
November 2009	Filmed behind the scenes at a model shoot/fashion show	*Bullet Boy* (*Saul Dibb 2004*), *Rolling with the*
April 2010	Filmed behind the scenes at a video shoot	*Nines* (*Julian Gilbey 2006*)
July 2010	Filmed behind the scenes at a video shoot Interviews with Andrew, Bernard and John	and *Dubplate Drama* (*Luke Hyams 2005*)
July–September 2010	Worked with Edward on London Development Agency funded project for young people aged 14–19 who are NEET	
October 2010 – ongoing	Identifying YouTube and Twitter presence for informants	
March 2011–July 2011	Filmed interviews – Adam, Victor, Quentin and Colin	
November 2011	Behind the scenes at video shoot. Filmed interviews with David, Eric, Fiona, Gillian, Harvey	
November 2012	Filmed interview with Steven	

Reciprocity and collaboration

Once I had immersed myself in this world, I became increasingly aware that I had a responsibility to articulate the context of the setting and also to ensure that wherever possible informants were not put at a disadvantage by participating in this research. They were, after all, giving up their time. This is a sector that operates on shoestring budgets, and as a business owner and an academic, I had access to resources and could draw on skills and experience that could support the business activities of my informants. Reciprocation in this context meant giving back, if requested, for something that I had received. So, if I had conducted an interview and the participant then asked for a service that I could provide, then I did so. In terms of collaboration, this involved working together and ongoing discussion to produce a piece of work (Lassiter 2005). Examples of this are the radio advertisement that Edward created for the Flex project I was working on for the London Development Agency (White 2013a). I had developed Flex in 2010 as an innovative response to a request from the now defunct London Development Agency. It was a project that aimed to prevent young people from becoming or remaining NEET. It was delivered in a variety of locations, mainly in the inner east London boroughs. Young people had the opportunity to undertake work experience and work placements, enrol on apprenticeships, undertake further training and develop business or self-employment opportunities.

The starting point for the reciprocal arrangements was when Diane asked me if I knew of a venue where she could shoot her 2008 Christmas calendar. I had some spare capacity in my office. In return, she let me go behind the scenes and take photographs as she prepared to shoot her calendar. Victor also invited me to an event he was performing at in east London. Victor asked for, and was provided with, a set of photographs that he could use for promotional and marketing purposes. In addition, I created a behind-the-scenes film of a music video shoot, an edited version of which was used on the informants' website. One artist needed a biography for the website he was creating for his business, so I drafted this for him. In addition, I proofread a Companies House application to establish a limited company for Andrew. Since the start of this research project, I have arranged various photo shoots and have provided the respondents with professional quality photographs.

Several months after his interview, Adam asked if one of our graphic designers could create a logo and design a CD cover for his forthcoming album. I arranged this for him. I also introduced this same MC to a training provider that works directly with Channel AKA and offers much sought-after music courses, and provided a reference to support his application.

Conducting the interviews

I planned to interview the respondents at two local community centres in Newham. This was sometimes possible. But I realised that I had to act immediately once I had permission for an interview. The respondents' mobile telephone numbers and contact details changed frequently. As a consequence, I missed two interviews (one with a singer and one with an MC) because I was arranging a time slot at the community centre. I became aware that a flexible approach was paramount and I had to be willing to carry out the interviews in whatever location the respondent wanted. I was accompanied on every visit that was not at the community centre.

From the literature review and the other research activities, I established a basic list of questions for the semi-structured interviews. It became apparent that the interviews could not be too long for fear of coming across like an official interview (Jobcentre, police or teachers). I devised a questionnaire and participant consent form and I carefully explained the purpose of my research. I kept the set questions to a minimum to make the interviews less formal. My aim was to undertake a ten- to fifteen-minute interview with each respondent. Respondents were not restricted to answering the questions listed. If something interesting arose, then I explored it further; for example, the concept of getting paid and making money was a key motivation, not just for its own sake but also as an outwardly visible measure of success. While I did not have a specific question about this, I ensured that where possible it formed part of the discussion, without asking respondents to reveal detailed information about their income.

I also made sure that I knew something about the respondents and their work or both before the interview as this helped the flow of the conversation, particularly as I do not fit the usual demographic for a grime fan. I asked direct, simple questions and reminded respondents before the start of each interview that they did not have to answer any question that they felt uncomfortable with and that the interview would be tape-recorded. Some respondents chose to have a friend with them.

I used a digital tape recorder for the first eleven UK interviews. I then downloaded each file to a laptop and transcribed the interview verbatim, with identifying details removed from the transcript. At the end of each interview, I recorded biographical details, context and location. I then analysed each transcript analysed and coded it for key motivations.

I undertook the Ayia Napa interviews in the field recorded them on film and transcribed them verbatim. The purpose of the fieldwork was to try to get a sense of what was going on. I had to change the research strategy slightly because it was not appropriate, in this setting, for me to ask questions about experiences of school, so I omitted these (Wolcott 2005). I edited the film from the Ayia Napa field trip into a forty-minute documentary, *Making It Funky* (White 2013b).

Conducting participant observation

My idea for participant observation arose out of my initial literature and video research. As Geertz suggests, the aim of participant observation is to produce a 'thick description' of social interaction in natural settings (Geertz 1973, p. 1). It was therefore important for me to be in the places where the music was played, performed and enjoyed, as well as for me to observe how this creative practice

– such as videos and radio programmes – is crafted and assembled. Participant observation can provide a flexible approach that enables the researcher to react to events and follow leads. Over time, it became apparent to me that a key focus for the participants in this social world was the summer season in the resort of Ayia Napa in southern Cyprus.

It was not possible for me to accept a role within the social situation being studied, as this social realm appeared to be predominantly male and under the age of forty. It was also important to consider the interviewer effect – as a 40-something-year-old female, who was older than all participants. Also, the social position of the researcher could enhance or inhibit rapport depending on the background of the informant (Skeggs *et al.* 2008). Furthermore, I had to demonstrate a shared knowledge of the subject to establish a relationship and have enough credibility with the respondents that they would want to talk to me and answer my questions.

I spent many months identifying and talking to key informants – becoming visible and allowing people to get used to seeing me around – before I could even start to ask any questions. I had to develop, nurture and maintain relationships with the respondents. In time, respondents made suggestions about who I should talk to and where to go next. Wherever possible and with permission, I took photographs and collected promotional material. For example, during the period of carrying out the primary research, I started to be invited to various events, where my respondents were performing or participating. At the start of my project the interviews were audio recordings, but over time it became apparent that this is an industry in which participants expect to be recorded on film; therefore interviews 1 to 11 are audio, and all subsequent interviews are filmed. I recorded all of the Ayia Napa interviews on film and then edited them into a forty-minute documentary, *Making It Funky*.

Writing ethnography

The role of the ethnographer is to study the group under observation and then translate or interpret what is going on and report back. Once this is done, writing up follows, and the ethnographer needs to decide how to tell the story. How does the researcher represent what has been observed and recorded? In this project, I made field notes, took photographs and made films. I have reflected on what I think I have observed and made a decision about what to include and what to omit. I have also reflected on the impact of my presence in the field.

What is included and what is omitted as well as the target audience are key considerations at the writing up stage. According to Van Maanen, whether the target audience is academic or the general population will have an impact on the format of the writing up, but common configurations include realist tales, confessional tales and impressionist tales (2011). Realist narratives offer a representation of the culture being studied that is a documentary style claim for authenticity. In this model, quotes from transcripts are offered straight form the horse's mouth. The inhabitants of the culture under study have their say through the author's pen. Confessional tales, on the other hand, offer stories of infiltration and demonstrate the process by which rapport was established with the respondents. The confessional tale is a blurred account, and the nature of the object of study cannot be taken for granted (Van Maanen 2011).

The ethnography in this research project utilises aspects of the realist and confessional positions. However, the documentary *Making It Funky* makes no claims to authenticity. It is an attempt to allow the respondents to give an account of themselves using different modes of articulation (Skeggs *et al.* 2008, p. 7).

Reflections on method

It has not been possible to simply observe what the participants are doing and how they are doing it, because this suggests a detachment that would have hindered the collection of data. My informants warmed to me because I understood the genre, without judging, and the interest and regard I had for their work was genuine and not for academic purposes only. One of the activities that still separated us was the dissemination of creative output. I wanted to explore what it felt like to create and broadcast a piece of film and then hope that people would watch it. I therefore created and uploaded a YouTube video of a conference presentation at Stanford University on my research area (MrCordice 2011) and asked for comments via Twitter. I hoped that the people I interviewed would watch it, and anticipated forty views. What I had not expected was that some or all of the respondents would retweet the video link because they wanted to broadcast what they saw as a history of grime. I even had comments from a grime MC in Italy. At the time of writing, this video has been viewed 1,300 times.

Getting in, finding out and then relaying that to those deemed to be 'outside' of that particular social world is a key component of the fieldworker's task, whether it was in the company of the former DJs who now sold an essentialised version of black identity instead of music and its by-products, or at a video shoot or nightclub event. Nevertheless, the types of events that I participated in with this group who considered themselves to be teachers, was because I was viewed as a 'sister' by that group. Even though I did not conform to their sartorial norms – I have dreadlocks but I do not cover my hair – also, the women in this setting always wore long skirts or dresses. This group allowed me in because I had been invited by Fred and because I paid the five pounds entrance fee, but the audience and teachers remained wary of my presence.

The use of video to record interviews and field research was a methodological turn that started in Ayia Napa, when it became evident that my informants were operating in a world where film was the standard currency. A transition therefore occurred from audio to a variety of video methods; large HD camera, mini HD camera and a laptop. These videos are supplemented with a written transcript for each interview. Like Sarah Pink, I make no distinction between 'old school' video, which is traditionally used as archive to be viewed by academic audiences, and 'cinema' or 'creative' film, which tells a story, because this difference, according to Sarah Pink, is not clear-cut (Pink 2006, p. 170). A realist reading of the facts does not hold true, because an objective reading is not possible. Throughout the field research phase, I created different types of film, for example, 'behind the scenes' or backstage documentaries and short clips that informants could use for their own creative purposes.

I did not just want to collect data; I wanted to be a part of this social world that was the object of study and work in partnership with the participants and creative practitioners, even if it was temporary. My films and photographs are not objective records; I cannot take myself out of it. My presence alters the dynamic of the situation whether I am asking questions or not.

The hierarchy between words and pictures is disrupted here. As Pink eloquently argues, academic meanings given to visual images are arbitrary, and ethnographers are subjective readers – personal experience and knowledge inform meaning. The visual data I have collected is not a representation of the field of inquiry; rather, it is one aspect of an articulation of the experiences and contexts of being a participant in the urban music economy. The interviews and the tangible artefacts combined with the visual data is an attempt to situate and communicate the feel of this social world.

Conclusion

I have outlined the methods that I used to design and undertake this research project. I began by rearticulating the original research question and examined why an ethnographic approach of semi-structured interviews and participant observation was deemed to be most suitable. I proceeded with an account of the research participants/informants in the study. Finally, I outlined how the study was conducted, detailing activities and timescales. My participation in the field of enquiry is made transparent and explicit. I am clearly creating, adding and ascribing meaning to activities.

It was important to see at first hand how the participants operated in this field. I was researching familiar ground, urban east London, but through an unfamiliar lens. Paul Willis excluded the experiences of the 'substantial West Indian and Asian minorities' in his study *Learning to Labour*. In this project, I have foregrounded the experiences of those young people from marginalised communities. I shared common ground with my informants in terms of business activities, and I reciprocated where requested and where I had the necessary and relevant resources to do so. My research is designed to explore a wide spread of activities and roles and elicit a personal account of what was important to them, thus ensuring that there is dialogue between me and the respondents.

The forty people I interviewed during five years of fieldwork were participants in the urban music economy as practitioners or consumers or both. Their practice disrupts accepted notions of what it means to be an entrepreneur and challenges the accepted notions of the NEET category.

Notes

1 The pirate radio stations referred to are those listed in October 2008 on www. transmissionzero.co.uk/radio/london-pirate-radio.
2 See also Westwood TV archive and others such as Mayhem TV, Risky Roads and SBTV.

References

alexgowers, 2006. *Blackjack ft Nasty – Girls Love Nasty*, Available at: www.youtube. com/watch?v=RirT6LigoxQ&feature=youtube_gdata_player [accessed 12 September 2010].

Atkinson, P., Coffey, A. and Delamont, S., 2003. *Key themes in qualitative research: Continuities and changes*, Walnut Creek, CA: Altamira Press.

Barnett, A., 2006. Gang videos glorify violence. *Guardian*. Available at: www.guardian. co.uk/uk/2006/oct/15/ukcrime.antonybarnett [accessed 9 July 2012].

Bourgois, P.I., 2003. *In search of respect: Selling crack in El Barrio*, Cambridge, UK and New York: Cambridge University Press.

De Castella, T., 2007. We talk to young people who have been involved in gangs. *Guardian*. Available at: www.guardian.co.uk/society/2007/nov/24/youthjustice. weekend [accessed 26 August 2010].

Drakopoulou Dodd, S. and Anderson, A.R., 2007. Mumpsimus and the mything of the individualistic entrepreneur. *International Small Business Journal*, 25(4), pp. 341–360.

Emerson, R.M., Fretx, R.I. and Shaw, L., 1995. *Writing ethnographic fieldnotes*, Chicago, IL: University of Chicago Press.

Geertz, C., 1973. *The interpretation of cultures*, New York, NY: Basic Books.

Glendinning, L., 2008. Two teenagers arrested over fatal stabbing of Shaquille Smith. *Guardian*. Available at: www.guardian.co.uk/uk/2008/sep/03/knifecrime.ukcrime [accessed 26 August 2010].

Hesmondhalgh, D. and Baker, S., 2011a. 'A very complicated version of freedom': Conditions and experiences of creative labour in three cultural industries. *Variant*, Spring (41).

Hesmondhalgh, D. and Baker, S., 2011b. *Creative labour: Media work in three cultural industries*, London and New York: Routledge.

Jansson, A., 2013. A second birth? Cosmopolitan media ethnography and Bourdieu's reflexive sociology. *International Journal of Cultural Studies*, 16(2), pp. 135–150.

Julian Gilbey, 2006. *Rollin with the Nines*, Flakjacket Films Ltd.

Katz, J., 2012. Ethnography's expanding warrants. *The Annals of the American Academy of Political and Social Science*, 642(1), pp. 258–275.

Koro-Ljungberg, M. and Greckhamer, T., 2005. Strategic turns labeled 'ethnography': From description to openly ideological production of cultures. *Qualitative Research*, 5(3), pp. 285–306.

Lassiter, L.E., 2005. *The Chicago guide to collaborative ethnography*, Chicago, IL: University of Chicago Press.

Luke Hyams, 2005. *Dubplate Drama*, Channel 4.

Menhaj Huda, 2006. *Kidulthood*, Cipher Films.

MrCordice, 2011. *Joy White grime research Stanford University 2011*. Available at: www.youtube.com/watch?v=Kmm-jZy2Bbg&feature=youtube_gdata_player [accessed 9 November 2011].

Noel Clarke, 2008. *Adulthood*, Cipher Films.

O'Grady, A., 2013. Interrupting flow: Researching play, performance and immersion in festival scenes. *Dancecult: Journal of Electronic Dance Music Culture*, 5 (Doing Nightlife and EDMC Fieldwork).

Pickering, M., 2008. *Research methods for cultural studies*, Edinburgh University Press.

Pink, S., 2006. *Doing visual ethnography: Images, media and representation in research*, 2nd edn, London, California, New Delhi, Singapore: Sage Publications.

playdirtymusic, 2011. *Konan & Krept – 4 Million Views (Official Video LOL)*. Available at: www.youtube.com/watch?v=SEoybZwGM-Q&feature=youtube_gdata_player [accessed 8 February 2012].

RealCharlieSloth, 2011. *Cashtastic – Fire In The Booth*. Available at: www.youtube.com/watch?v=8X2jOfYn6z4&feature=youtube_gdata_player [accessed 10 September 2011].

Richard Laxton, 2006. *Life and Lyrics*, United International Pictures.

Rose, A., 2008. Teenage knife and gun fatalities hit an all-time high. *The Guardian*. Available at: www.guardian.co.uk/world/2008/dec/28/knife-crime-deaths-eyewitness [accessed 9 July 2012].

Saul Dibb, 2004. *Bullet Boy*, BBC Films.

Skeggs, B., Thumim, N. and Wood, H., 2008. 'Oh goodness, I am watching reality TV': How methods make class in audience research. *European Journal of Cultural Studies*, 11(1), pp. 5–24.

Van Maanen, J., 2011. *Tales of the field: On writing ethnography*, Chicago, IL and London: University of Chicago Press.

White, J., 2013a. *Flex Ad_ Edward*. Available at: www.youtube.com/watch?v=q4y3Ljlri Ks&feature=youtube_gdata_player [accessed 28 November 2013].

White, J., 2013b. *Making It Funky*. Available at: www.youtube.com/watch?v=ZBmZg2l6 7qU&feature=youtube_gdata_player [Accessed 28 November 2013].

Willis, P.E., 1993. *Learning to labour: How working class kids get working class jobs*, Aldershot: Ashgate.

Willis, P.E., 2006. Symbolic creativity. In *Cultural theory and popular culture: A reader*. University of Georgia Press, p. 657.

Wilson, W.J. and Chaddha, A., 2009. The role of theory in ethnographic research. *Ethnography*, 10(4), pp. 549–564.

Wolcott, H.F., 2005. *The art of fieldwork*, Walnut Creek, CA: Altamira Press.

Index

Page numbers in *italics* denote tables, those in **bold** denote figures.